CW00670370

A REFLECTIVE GUIDE TO GENDER IDENTITY COUNSELLING

of related interest

Counselling Skills for Working with
Gender Diversity and Identity
Michael Beattie and Penny Lenihan with Robin Dundas
ISBN 978 1 78592 741 6
eISBN 978 1 78450 481 6
Part of the Essential Skills for Counselling series

Theorizing Transgender Identity for Clinical Practice
A New Model for Understanding Gender
S.J. Langer
ISBN 978 1 78592 765 2
eISBN 978 1 78450 642 1

How to Understand Your Gender
A Practical Guide for Exploring Who You Are
Alex Iantaffi and Meg-John Barker
Foreword by S. Bear Bergman
ISBN 978 1 78592 746 1
eISBN 978 1 78450 517 2

Counseling Transgender and Non-Binary Youth
The Essential Guide
Irwin Krieger
ISBN 978 1 78592 743 0
eISBN 978 1 78450 482 3

A REFLECTIVE GUIDE TO
GENDER IDENTITY COUNSELLING

MADISON-AMY WEBB (MBACP) ACC

Jessica Kingsley *Publishers*
London and Philadelphia

First published in 2019
by Jessica Kingsley Publishers
73 Collier Street
London N1 9BE, UK
and
400 Market Street, Suite 400
Philadelphia, PA 19106, USA

www.jkp.com

Copyright © Madison-Amy Webb 2019

All rights reserved. No part of this publication may be reproduced in any material form (including photocopying, storing in any medium by electronic means or transmitting) without the written permission of the copyright owner except in accordance with the provisions of the law or under terms of a licence issued in the UK by the Copyright Licensing Agency Ltd. www.cla.co.uk or in overseas territories by the relevant reproduction rights organisation, for details see www.ifrro.org. Applications for the copyright owner's written permission to reproduce any part of this publication should be addressed to the publisher.

Warning: The doing of an unauthorised act in relation to a copyright work may result in both a civil claim for damages and criminal prosecution.

Library of Congress Cataloging in Publication Data
A CIP catalog record for this book is available from the Library of Congress

British Library Cataloguing in Publication Data
A CIP catalogue record for this book is available from the British Library

ISBN 978 1 78592 383 8
eISBN 978 1 78450 733 6

Printed and bound in Great Britain

MIX
Paper from
responsible sources
FSC
www.fsc.org   FSC® C013056

Dedicated to my dearest Boo.
And Mhorag, thank you for your belief in me.

Disclaimer

One function of this book is to clarify the confusion that exists around language and gender variance. The author has used the word 'transsexual' for acknowledging one such permutation of gender variance with which a client may present in therapy. Other variations are discussed throughout the book. In this case a transsexual client is more likely, but not exclusively, to be someone requiring certain elements of medical interventions to support their transition. The author acknowledges that the word 'transsexual' can be outdated and upsetting to some people, and its inclusion here is not intended in any way to cause offence. It is worth noting that any practitioners working with gender variant clients are advised to ask the client how they wish to be regarded and the appropriate pronouns to use when addressing them.

CONTENTS

ACKNOWLEDGEMENTS

Many individuals have contributed to the production of this book in many differing ways.

Firstly, I would like to thank Tina, my partner, wife, soul mate. You alone have truly come to know me, and my essence, irrespective of where I am on the continuum. You have confirmed to me that it is possible to truly love the spirit of someone for who they are, irrespective of the outside presentation; and I am blessed to be with you in this life. All my love for the rest of our days.

Thank you to Jennie Penkul, for her tireless work in giving the chapters their first read through and her amazing ability in suggesting alterations without actually saying so – a true miracle worker!

I would like to thank Joan Roughgarden PhD for her assistance in the chapter regarding gender diversity in nature, and for allowing me to use some material from her research work.

I would also extend my deepest appreciation to Dr J. Hayes-Light for their assistance with the chapter that includes intersexuality, and for allowing me to use website material within this book.

I would like to give my upmost respect and thanks to my clients, wherever they sit upon the gender continuum. There is much truth in the saying that you may not get the clients you want, but you get the ones that teach you something about yourself.

I would like to thank the therapists and supervisors who have worked with me over the years, in particular Sanja Oakley, Martin Schmidt, Philip Boddey and Dilly's Phipps. You have walked with me during the chapters of my journey and equipped me to undertake the next chapter. For this I'm appreciative and feel fortunate to have known and spent time with you. Thank you – you are truly rare colleagues within the profession.

I would also like to thank Diana Flanigan. Without your input I can honestly say I wouldn't be involved with the work I am at this stage of my career. Your involvement has taught me to trust in myself and to recognise what I have to offer.

I would like to thank my family. Some tough lessons have taken place during our time together, including those which have continued to leave me with strong feelings. Notwithstanding this, I am ever appreciative of how these events have aided my personal growth and progress and can only hope you were able to take something positive from them too.

And finally, but certainly not least, I want to thank my good friend Carolyn who has shown me that family doesn't always have to be blood-related. Some of the most accepting people have come from the most unexpected places.

PREFACE

This book began life as 'Debunking Gender', a training manual for counsellors, psychotherapists and professionals whose working roles brought them into contact with gender variant (GV) and trans clients. Whilst developing the training day, I was keen to create something other than the usual dull procession of PowerPoint slides. I wanted Debunking Gender to convey something more of a reflective, lived experience of gender identity (GI), so it became an experiential event, with explorative personal exercises around individuals' understanding of their GI, a series of personal monologues (drawn from my exploration of my gender within therapy), and a space for attendees to consider something that most of us accept without question. The training was to all intents and purposes a very different Continuing Professional Development experience than that which professionals are used to. At the core of the training there were two fundamental messages to convey to the attendees. Firstly, that diverse GI is universal and affects us all, irrespective of whether we've given it consideration or not. I felt at the time – as I still do – that some level of self-reflection of one's gender is fundamental for a clinical practitioner, regardless of whether they are going to work with GV clients or not. This self-reflective enquiry leads us to the essence of who we are. Back in 2013, GV was still very much off the public's radar. It wasn't until pop culture's hyper-fascination with transsexual Caitlin Jenner's public transition in the USA that GV began to be pulled, kicking and screaming, once more into the public spotlight. It had happened once before – 40 years earlier – when another US transsexual, Christine Jorgensen, beguiled the world's media. Jorgensen's impact on public interest was short-lived; however, her impact on many other closeted transsexuals was long-lasting and gave them hope for possibly being able to be their true selves.

In recent years, media attention hasn't always been positive or helpful. So, my second goal for debunking gender was to clarify what GV is and isn't. As has been seen throughout history, GV has always existed in many forms, and we have had clear examples in recent years of how awareness can lead to widespread public misunderstandings, misconceptions and fear. Barely a day goes by without some story or article appearing in the media about the difficulties that *gender binary* (see Glossary of Terms) people in society have in believing GV to be real or even valid. This in turn raises questions of how a society that has been brought up on the false truth that gender binary (male or female) is the only authentic GI can accommodate the needs of GV people into the current social structure – for example, which toilets should a GV person use when out in public? Lack of understanding and acceptance of everyday issues affecting GV people has created a very uncertain and distressing place for them to be living in.

By the time I was approached to write this book (early in 2017), the furore around GV had reached such a crescendo that at times it felt like parts of society were really against those who didn't fit into the binary, and (dare I say it?) there have been actual displays of hatred towards GV people. What kept nagging away in my mind was that a lot of the problems around gender stemmed from the continual misuse of language, caused partly by the sustained misinterpretation of the nature of GV. The main culprits here are journalists and article writers whose lack of knowledge of GV perpetuates the status quo. This constant display of confusion cried out for these matters to be a central component of my book. I began reflecting on the accomplishments and integrations that GV has established since 2013 and on where GI's evolution is headed in the future, and this was the starting point for me in my book proposal.

To achieve my goals, rather than getting embroiled in media chatter, I had to cut through the hysteria and allow myself time to study the actual facts around gender diversity – it's essential to gather information to challenge the black-and-white thinking that GV doubters rely upon, as this will certainly impact on GV clients who may have been challenged over their status. It became crucial for me to demonstrate the need for reliable facts – for example, we have tangible evidence that GV occurs in many animal species; also the Bible, the Koran and the Torah all have references accepting what we now acknowledge as GV, and demonstrating that multiple genders were not just accepted but had an acknowledged place within their theological beliefs. Finally, there is now neurological evidence to corroborate the idea that GV is more than a personal choice.

During the writing of this book I maintained a professional balance between keeping an eye on what is happening out in the world (to ensure the book is current and relevant), yet at the same time not allowing myself to get caught up in hysteria. This is something I would urge you as counsellors and other professionals to maintain, since confusion is potent and likely to hinder your client work (our clients might already be confused enough about the external situations they find themselves in).

Finally, I wanted to mention the experiential exercises. These have always been a significant part of my training sessions and are insightful and engaging for the attendees. I wanted to give all readers the chance to experience this for themselves, and also to provide them with a space to gently challenge and examine what is at the core of who we are and what informs our knowledge of that experience. Counsellors and psychotherapists working with GV who have not explored their own GI as part of their initial training could be putting themselves at a disadvantage when sitting opposite a client whose experience of their GI appears a million miles from themselves.

So often in modern society we are expected to keep considering diversity. Well, in the case of this book I am going to ask you to reassess and to now place an emphasis on the personal similarities with yourself and your fellow members of the human species!

INTRODUCTION

'Congratulations! It's a boy/girl!' There it is: the moment our sex is assigned to us.

In that moment, how we will be treated and the role we will be expected to perform within society have been set. Also, in that moment – and it usually occurs without question – we are implanted in a social group (our family), and all the expectations and dynamics that go with being part of it are laid firmly and unknowingly upon our shoulders. Sometimes these are explicit, but for the most part they are not. Either way we transgress them at our peril!

As children, our future selves are shaped by our family and the dynamics of the interactions that we are exposed to. The hidden legacies of the relationships that our parents had with their parents (our grandparents) – which they may have struggled with, and been shaped by – now become our inheritance. Benign as some of them might be, passing quietly into the memory of our childhood, there are those that are malignant 'conditions of worth': the things we think we must meet for other people to consider us worthy of their love, positive regard or acceptance. As children, we learn that there are certain things we do that please our parents or caregivers, and we strive to do those things, often to the detriment of our true selves. We may, for example, feel intimidated by family members to conform and be acceptable and worthy of love. These 'legacy judgements' attach themselves to us and refuse to become part of us without at first changing us from our innate path, or what Carl Rogers called our 'Organismic Self' (our innate and true self).

As we enter our teens and twenties, we find ourselves trying to find our place in the world, and growing our identity at the same time as we are coming to terms with the physical and chemical changes taking place within us. Family pressures can make adolescence an especially difficult and painful time in this respect – whilst maintaining our levels of acceptability to family and peers, we feel internal pressure to spread our wings and be who we naturally are.

For some of us, adolescence harbours something inexplicable. As we go through our teenage years, we experience sensations or catch momentary glimpses of something uncanny within ourselves: something strange that doesn't quite make sense. It feels like part of us, but our brains tell us something different – something we might feel ashamed of – and worries about personal acceptability enter the forefront of our minds. The phenomena carry an unacceptable gravity: guilt and maybe even self-hatred. What's more, because of what it might mean, we must treat its presence as a dirty secret that cannot be shared with anyone. For surely to admit this about ourselves will mean we are perverted, corrupted and likely to be damned and cast out from society? At the very least it will mean we are not quite following the acceptable narrative of how to be and live our life.

Regardless of whether we deny its existence or become curious as to what it means for us, the one certain thing is that it will remain part of us throughout our life. We can bury these feelings under a more acceptable Western heterosexual narrative; however, as we try to give our all to this narrative, there is the likelihood that we may experience a dissonance between the choices we've made regarding how we are living our life and the internal pressures experienced as uncanny. By uncanny I am referring to a fleeting sense of what might or what we might be. We may experience it almost like catching sight of something, but not being sure what it is or even if we experienced it at all.

What happens next is usually the point at which I first encounter the individual trying to make sense of themselves – the focus of this book, their GI. The individual may have a sense of what is going on or they may be utterly fearful of this reoccurring part of themselves, this rogue element that just won't fit within their normality or leave them in peace. Their experience and language are extremely personal and I as their therapist am mindful not to go wading into their world imposing my interpretations upon them and the occurrence they are experiencing. There will be confusion – a lot of confusion – as the reality of their personal narrative unfolds and the possible outcomes of the future begin to manifest; fear for their future begins to solidify. In a Western heteronormative society, with its neurotic belief in a binary view of GI, the individual who strays from the path and ploughs their own furrow by identifying as anything other than the '*social norm*' is challenging the existence of that so-called 'social norm' and that can come with a heavy price tag. Why? Well, because we in our Western heteronormative societies are brought into the world to take the gender binary as an unchallengeable truth. There are men and there are women. There are penises and there are breasts and vaginas. End of. Just accept it!

Here are some precise clarifications regarding the terminology used in this book:

Sex: This is assigned at birth and is based on the physical genitals present at the time (penis or vagina). Sex can be male, female or intersex.

Gender identity (GI): This is regardless of our physical sex (penis, vagina, breast). Gender identity can be male, female or something else. It is how/who we sense or feel ourselves to be.

Sexuality: This is who we are sexually attracted to. It can be any permutation (i.e. heterosexual, homosexual, bisexual, polysexual, asexual or any other version of erotic attraction).

I hope you can now comprehend where the confusion around GI originates, and as we shall see as a species subscribing to this binary model we are classifying ourselves as not being as advanced in evolutionary terms as we usually consider ourselves to be; however, I shall put forward some reasons that there are those who would rather we maintain the limitations of the binary.

Personally speaking, while I know I was born into the world and brought up/conditioned for societal life as a male, my homing instinct was all the while reminding me of my innate and true self through my experience of the uncanny feeling about my own GI. I would not consider relinquishing my own gender furrow and returning to the pseudo balance of the binary.

Reflections

Throughout this book, I will walk with you much like I do with the many clients I've worked with over the years and will take a path which doesn't just take the binary blindly. I will also reflect upon personal experiences from significant stages of my own journey in understanding and reconciling my GI. If you'll indulge me for a minute, an example is the following anecdote which took place in the 1980s when I was 11 or 12 years old. I remember regularly reading an agony aunt column in a daily tabloid paper (looking back, I can see my interest in the struggles people have during their lives as they wrestle with being in the world!). One day a letter caught my eye. It had been sent in by a young man in his twenties who was trapped between living his life as a regular red-blooded man (he loved his football, his beer, and had a girlfriend) yet he carried a dark and worrisome secret. If his friends and family found out about it, he was sure to be shamed and rejected by society. His secret was that he loved to dress in female clothes. Not just that, he knew that sneaking into his girlfriend's underwear and whatever else that fitted him wasn't enough. He owned a thought, and however much he might try to deny its existence, he knew it was part of him, but its very presence carried so much guilt and shame that he wanted to reject or abandon the thought in any way he could. Crossdressing had released the genie from the bottle and he now wanted to look like a girl; and if such a reality could ever happen, he wanted to be a girl. What was he to do? The agony aunt was very sensitive and her reply was surprisingly considered, seeing how in later years this tabloid went on to vilify trans people with insensitive headlines and freak-show-styled stories. I imagined this agony aunt sitting this terrified young man down and putting into words a rational explanation of what he might be experiencing. As she spoke to him, I felt like she was talking to me. She introduced me to words that made my blood run cold. There were a lot of similarities between his story and things I already had a sense of, and she spoke about urges associated with clothing and the feeling of being the opposite sex (my uncanny). I came to learn that some of his behaviour and mine (the dressing in female clothes) was called 'transvestism' and that both he and I were probably transvestites. And as if that wasn't enough, if he had feelings about being female, the typical phrase *de jour* was 'a woman trapped in a man's body'. The conclusion was that he might be *'transsexual'* and could seek medical assistance to medically transition. I slowly put that paper down and, although I had gained a possible understanding, I felt I had been sentenced to carry my own dark secret.

Back in the 1980s the terms 'transgender', 'trans' and 'gender variance' didn't exist; nor did 'gender dysphoria'. Transsexuality was classed as a mental illness (Gender Identity Disorder in the *Diagnostic and Statistical Manual* – DSM) and transvestism was regarded as a paraphilia (a condition in which a person's sexual arousal and gratification depend on fantasising about, and engaging in, sexual behaviour that is atypical and extreme). These were the days before the worldwide web, and getting your hands on reliable information was incredibly difficult. What was also challenging was that without some of the understandings we have now, the GV individual was left to flounder in a world where their behaviours were wrongly understood according to a short-sighted and judgemental diagnosis. If you didn't fit into what was considered normal, then you must be ill because that was what the medical literature at the time stated.

From 2014, things improved, but only marginally, when understanding began to accommodate a position in the world for people who felt uncomfortable with the relationship they had between their body and the GI they sensed themselves as having. There was now recognition that the relationship between the two could cause mental distress and impact on the individual's mental well-being, and the term 'gender dysphoria' was introduced.

Although this was progress, it was limiting and prescriptive in that now people who experienced 'gender dysphoria' all seemed to look at the symptomology of the condition and describe what they were experiencing in accordance with a tick list. In other words, with the arrival of the template for a diagnosis, there was no space for an individual's unique experience.

Many times over the years I have reflected on the experiences which have led me to the conclusion of a personal GV; and whilst I can look at the *DSM* symptomology for gender dysphoria, it has always fallen short in clarifying my experiences, which left me feeling on the outside of the diagnosis, in much the same way the phrase 'a woman trapped in a man's body' left me feeling. If anything, I felt oddly further away from myself rather than clarifying my understanding of self. This would many years later become a fundamental aspect of the work I was to undertake within my own development and also with my GV clients.

When I now try to provide some sort of a definition of how I experienced gender dysphoria, it is more about a recognition of a self I can never be, at least not in a biological sense. Sociologically, I am at the mercy of those I meet during my day-to-day life, if they recognise enough of the visual cues I provide for them to interpret what they see in my presentation as a representation of femininity. Regardless of how well I pass as female day to day, I am still troubled daily by dysphoria. Some days are better than others. However, I can still sense that, regardless of what I have undertaken and included as part of my physical/medical transition, I will never be a biological female from birth and I will not have had the full range of female experiences. I recognise that the feelings I experience in those reoccurring moments are a form of repeating grief. Freud spoke of how our dreams speak of how our psyche (unconscious life) is astonishingly mobile and adventurous, even if our lived life is not (Freud 2001). Just reflect for a moment on all the places you have gone to in your dreams… the storylines you might have had, the people you might have been, the relationships you might have had, the people you were attracted to, and who was attracted to you. Maybe you are shocked by what went through your mind and maybe you would never share your dreams with anyone on account of guilt and fear that they might find you socially unacceptable. Freud considered that in our unconscious life we are bisexual even if we never engage with this on the physical plane (Rapoport 2009). It's as if we don't have the courage to even acknowledge those instincts which exist in the dark recesses of our mind, let alone dare to engage with them. We try to play it safe in life and take the line of least resistance by attempting to ground these ego-driven aspects of ourselves; thus we can engage in living solely in what we interpret as the 'real' (safer) version of our world.

I have often wondered if some people enjoy dressing up in costume or fancy-dress as a form of escapism from playing it safe in their everyday lives. This might allow them to access parts of themselves they would be ashamed to incorporate as part of their socially acceptable self; or maybe they get to play with a narrative they feel attracted too. Either way, this is something very different to GV, because underpinning dressing up in costume is a transient self-expression, rather than the fixed self-concept of GI. Consider the public's over-interest in the physical aspect of transition, for example effemimania (the cultural obsession with anything focused on male femininity, which is underpinned by traditional sexism and the view that femininity is inferior to masculinity). Here we find ourselves dealing with matters of disbelief: Would a man really give up his social privileges? And dressing up as a woman is one thing, but considering aspects of a medical transition is something else. There must be something so pressing and so painful for someone to seemingly risk so much.

I've concluded that I recognise that gender dysphoria is like Freud's unconscious bisexuality. When people experience gender dysphoria, they acknowledge that there is more to them than what is on the surface. Like the proverbial iceberg, moments of dysphoria that thread through the individual's days (myself included) are reminders that the person is incomplete; the fundamental aspect of their self is hidden, with only glimpses of their essence known – a cruel disparity between biology, psychology and social conditioning that leaves the individual with a seemingly unhealable schism. Conditions of self-worth (being acceptable and liked by those around the individual) and the small matter of keeping themselves safe mean that any open acknowledgement of their GI discord is not an option. I have recognised through my clinical work with GV clients that their gender dysphoria is experienced in a variety of ways and interpreted by all of the senses. Yet ultimately, what is within the essence of the expression of gender dysphoria is the recognition that the person is not what they wish themselves to be, and in that moment there is usually such an overwhelming sense of loss that their very existence can feel threatened. It's as if the dysphoria creates an inner state of 'How can I be expected to continue living when that life will not be as I truly am?'

The GV individual is blighted by uncontrollable episodes of repeated grief and mourning throughout their life whenever the dysphoria is triggered. Grief and mourning are a universal language which we are all bonded by. We have all had someone/something in our life which ceases to be physically part of it, consigning us to the arrival of a void. Some people block this out through fear of their very existence being swallowed, while others stare into it and wonder how they will ever be the same again. For the GV individual this grief repeats, and repeats, and repeats; day after day they are stuck in an endless cycle of reoccurring loss. Unlike regular grief at the loss of a loved one or a precious thing, the grief of the GV individual has no stages to pass through, leading to a healthy reconciliation with this internal conflict. The only option in alleviating the repeating turmoil is for them to manifest into the real world the essence of who they truly are. I am aware that I have used the term 'gender dysphoria' several times, but I have not yet indicated how it manifests itself. I will share what *I* experienced (which is unique to me); however, having talked with clients, I can confirm that there are similarities in our experiences of this phenomenon.

Typically, I would be involved in my daily commitments – there was never any specific mood or frame of mind which would make me more susceptible to an episode of dysphoria – but if I was in a low mood I would find the dysphoria made a bigger impact upon me and it was usually harder to manage the rest of my day due to the emotional distraction. My partner would describe this as if I was walking with a stone in my shoe that I wasn't allowed to remove; I was expected to just keep on with this painful distraction gnawing away at me.

The trigger would be seeing a female, either in an image or physically present. The females would all be different – for me this wasn't about a type, and I wish to clarify here that what I'm describing is very different to sexual attraction, where a man may fix his gaze upon a female and she in that moment becomes the erotic trigger/focus of arousal for his sexual desire or excitement. A slight variation to the female trigger would be observing a female-related activity. This would elicit the same sequence of events, as follows. There I would be, and the image and the expression of the female's femininity would trigger what I can best describe as a simultaneous thought/reactive feeling, as if out of nowhere I was struck by a voice from within me telling me in a disparaging tone: 'You will *never* be like her!' In that same moment I usually found the light dimmed and the outside world disappeared. Then I was hit with what I can best describe as a hot flush. However, this was a physical hot flush coupled with a psychological wash of utter dread and desperation somewhat like the experience of a panic attack. I would be frozen physically, stopped dead in my tracks, although in my head it would be a cacophony of images and colours collapsing and fading in on one another as an emotional tsunami washed inwards to my very core. Then a moment of cold deadness as the emotional gravity brought a backwash of stultifying melancholy through me, with the flotsam and jetsam of phrases snagging and stinging: 'How can I be expected to continue living when that life will not be as I truly am?' and 'I want to be her, not have her.' Then the lights came on and I was back in the present, with the only trace of the dysphoric episode being the phrases swilling around in my internal world for the remainder of the day. An episode such as this could occur at any time and be repeated any number of times. For the GV individual these episodes will vary, but I've noted a similar structure and elements to what I've described above in all the other descriptions I've been given.

Let us go back to the young man from the agony aunt story. It is very clear that GV people have many shared experiences. They are all unique, yet there are certain stages each one of us goes through in finding the natural place we inhabit within our congruent self in relation to GI or some other aspect of ourselves. The experience of living, by its very temperament, knocks us off course, in that each time we encounter a 'condition of worth' or are criticised for something we do or are, we drift that little bit further away from our organismic natural self. The paradox is that for us all 'being in the world' signifies that we cannot help being influenced and changed by others and society (I would add by what we might consider positive and negative phenomena). It is probable that we will drift away from our congruent self, and that is the nature of being in the world as a child and at the mercy of the adults responsible for us. Therefore, what I have identified as the 'uncanny' phenomenon could be a homing instinct from this congruent self, endeavouring to catch our attention and guide us towards that part of ourselves which we have drifted far away from.

There are several aspects of GI which I will address within this book. Most issues that clients bring into the consulting room benefit from addressing the 'back story', the *where*, the *when* and the *how* of the client's experience (their wish to make some sense of what they are experiencing). For a client whose presenting concerns are GI-based, this is no less an important line of exploration. However, as we shall see, there are several larger influences which will be affecting what the person experiences from family, society and the wider world in which they live. To this end, I will be devoting Part 1 of the book to an examination of the 'back story' of GI in the wider context, as natural science (in particular, evolutionary theory), religion, sociology and cultural evolution have all played a role and are shaping the GI landscape we are currently experiencing.

Part 1 will therefore explore these aspects and their impact on GI, not only for those questioning their GI but for all of us. We all have a GI and, as I stated earlier, most of us accept what we were assigned at birth without question. What I will propose within these pages is that the question of authentic GI is not just something affecting the trans population but every one of us, including you dear reader.

Part 2 will focus on the 'doing' of GI. GI is something that many people barely give a second thought to, yet it's fundamental, affecting many aspects of how we live. What we do and how we are expected to behave are reinforced through gender stereotypes from an early age, and this continues throughout our lives. Unless they are experiencing a dissonance with their GI, people tend to never question what they are told they are. What can be lost is a sense of personal GI creativity, and even a sense of being congruent. I mean, how do you begin to challenge what you have been told about your GI, and what can you do with your GI afterwards? It's all very well challenging the status quo, but what is there on the other side of this, how do you take ownership of your GI and what is likely to be the impact of this?

In Part 2 we will build upon what has been learnt about ourselves within the exercises in Part 1 and begin a reflective process with those discoveries. Personal reflectiveness is an integral part of the therapeutic process with clients exploring their GI, and it's just one of the interventions which is worth being mindful of not only with your clients but also yourself. Once we have studied the bigger problematic picture, it will become evident why a reflective process towards understanding GI is essential. We will explore why we in the West appear to have such a limited vocabulary in relation to doing GI, while seemingly less-developed cultures around the world have always had not only a richer vocabulary regarding GI, but also a healthier comprehension and recognition of the many ways we as a species can 'do' gender. The reflective process cannot undo what has come to pass through many generations of gender bias, but it can begin to undermine the damage that has been done, which has essentially knocked our collective (Western heteronormative) values off-course to the place where the individual is stricken from their place of being congruent and reaching their organismic self, to where we now exist with forms of gender apartheid/suppression, and trends such as effemimania.

Clear examples of how our beliefs around GI have been limited can be found when we consider gender order theory models such as 'emphasised femininity' and 'hegemonic masculinity'. Hegemonic masculinity perpetuates the dominant social position of men, ultimately resulting in the patriarchal society we have and the subordinate social position of women (later we will explore the differences between patriarchal and matriarchal society).

Hegemonic masculinity establishes the idea that any man who doesn't align with the notions of primary white masculinity is inferior. It aims for these hegemonic ultra-masculine men to be exclusive and hierarchically distinguished. Men brought up with the traditional male values of hegemonic masculinity (being tough, being powerful, showing aggression, whilst suppressing emotions which are considered weak or feminine) very often lead to men demanding the power in a relationship and having a domineering attitude.

Emphasised femininity is the idea that women must conform to the needs and desires of men. It confirms the idea that the ultimate reason for a woman's existence is to provide man with sexual validation, carry his babies, serve his household, be submissive and be sexually available to serve his needs. Girls who are raised within the values of emphasised femininity grow up to become submissive women and do not seek power in a relationship. They often find it unattractive for a man to treat them equally or seek their opinion in making decisions since the idea is planted deep within them that it's a man's role to lead and women should follow.

These outdated models of doing gender reinforce the equally outdated concept of the gender binary by affirming its validity and imposing it upon generation after sleepwalking generation. The gender binary demands the removal of gender individualism and social conformity. Of course, these versions of the binary are extreme, but they continually reinforce what we're told at birth through marketing and advertising day in and day out. Many of us hold some belief in them as our personal inevitability of how to be the sex we are and do our GI; maybe many of us have some of these qualities in a more diluted form – some men can be nurturing and emotional, while some women can be tough and emotionally detached. But what if we regard our GI as a blank canvas rather than a descriptive template with which we can describe and articulate what we believe to be the essence of ourselves, those uncanny glimpses? It will mean we can begin to understand ourselves and our GV clients better.

In this book I want to demonstrate that across our planet and throughout our societies there has always been GV; its lack of understanding can cause a perceived threat, and that's where problems arise.

The author, feminist and existentialist Simone de Beauvoir is often quoted as saying: 'One is not born, but rather becomes, a woman' (de Beauvoir 2011, p.283). What she was proposing is the old argument of nature versus nurture, or essentialism versus social construct, in how women become women (or indeed we could say, men become men). Maybe it might be more accurate to say: 'One isn't born, but rather becomes one's gender identity.'

Important Considerations

This book has been challenging to write for many reasons, mainly because the area of gender is in a state of unrest, which we will come to in due course within the book. The main reason for this is that we are living in a significant stage where Western heteronormativity is colliding with our understanding of GI, with ramifications for us all. However, for me to capture the zeitgeist is almost impossible because the collision and its unfolding consequences haven't run their course so my aim has been to capture the flavour of this time.

Having said this, I wish to address two points which are themes in my client work and they will run like threads throughout this book.

Firstly, during the writing process I have been mindful of the ever-changing climate within the media in relation to how GV is being portrayed. It is often misrepresented, and this happens mainly (although not exclusively) through the misleading use of language defining GV. I fully appreciate that what I am about to say next is likely to upset a good few individuals if they happen to read this, but I believe it needs to be said. Some of the individuals I'm referring to as being in part responsible for the current misleading portrayal of GV are themselves GV. There are some within this population who consider themselves to be trans activists, and there are others I've observed who have a limited or confused understanding of the subject. This second group of people come from within the media. I am not opposed to GV people grouping together to stand and encourage positive change in terms of rights and conditions for that section of the population who have been treated poorly not only by society but by those services which are there to support them.

I will explore the trans activists' activities later in the book, and also explore those whom I feel are confused over their possible GV; but right now I want to highlight what I consider to be one of the biggest shortcomings of these people and other parts of the media. It pertains to the misappropriation of language and the absolute confusion which exists as a result of the current misuse of the word 'transgender' and its abbreviated form 'trans'. The word was coined by psychiatrist John F. Oliven of Columbia University in 1965, and there is a history of gender campaigners borrowing it for their own ends; yet in recent history, and certainly up to the 2014–15 explosion of GV within society, the term was used as an umbrella to cover all forms of non-binary gender. People are not 'transgender' or 'trans' and there isn't a medical diagnosis of either. The constant misappropriation of the word has made it redundant. And this being the case, I have taken the decision that I will not use the word in this book – to do so would, I feel, be adding further to the chaos that exists as a result of its constant misuse. I have decided that I will instead use the term gender variant/variance (GV). These terms are relatively uncontaminated by misuse and they also are used as umbrella terms for gender diversity. I'm aware that UK government documentation for legal ruling uses 'gender variance' rather than 'transgender', which has now been tainted by pop culture and is rife with misunderstandings. My main concern is that the term is being used by cis people who don't have a full understanding(or don't care as long as they can sell their units of media) about the impact the misuse of the terms has on real people. I hope that, having read this book, you will be able to introduce others to these terms and encourage their use moving forward in the dispensing of your duties in relation to your GV clients. I will address this later in more depth, but I do recognise that the acronym 'LGBT' utilises the word, and I am not a supporter of its inclusion.

Over the last few years working with GV, including client work and training counsellors and psychotherapists, I have often found myself having conversations (whilst being only too aware of the difficulties of living openly with GV) about how this is a very exciting time to be involved and working in one of the last social themes of our time. There is huge social change – we are living at the rock face as GI is formed minute by minute, day by day, and month by month – and what happens now will affect us all. I'm not being overly dramatic when I say that, because even now as I write governments all over the world are considering their stance on GI legislation and changing their laws in accordance with that. What is important to recognise is that you don't have to be GV for this to be of significance to you. Whatever the outcomes of political and social change might be for gender, we can be sure that it will impact everyone, whether questioning their GI or not. I will invite you to explore through a series of exercises what it is you think you know about your GI. For how can we expect our clients to explore their GI if this isn't a path we are prepared to tread ourselves?

Secondly, I wish to propose the idea that in fact we are all a bit GV. Throughout this book I will demonstrate ways in which – from the micro to the macro, and physiologically to the physical – all our GIs may be different to how we think we identify. And it is my belief that terms like 'transgender' and 'trans' perpetuate the state of 'us and them'. Rather, I propose using 'gender variance' as an inclusive term for all GI as this is something which is relevant to every person. As we will see, GI is by its very nature diverse.

While I want to promote GI as being a universal GV, there will be times when I refer to GV with more of an inclination towards those who have already undertaken self-examination and sense themselves to be something other than what their birth sex says. I am well aware that this concept of universal GV becoming commonly accepted is something that might take many years before it has the slightest chance of becoming a possibility; I believe that all things that eventually become commonplace have small origins.

PART 1

THE GENESIS OF GENDER VARIANCE

All species have genetic diversity – their biological rainbow. No exceptions. Biological rainbows are universal and eternal. Yet biological rainbows have posed difficulties for biologists since the beginnings of evolutionary theory. The founder of evolutionary biology, Charles Darwin, details his own struggle to come to terms with natural variation in his diaries from *The Voyage of the Beagle*.

(Roughgarden 2004, p.13)

GLOSSARY OF TERMS

Please let's try to eliminate the main problem that surrounds GI (i.e. the misinterpretation and the misappropriation of relevant language). Rather than have the glossary of terms tucked away at the back of the book as something that you refer to if required, I am allowing myself to be informed by the years of delivering my training programmes on GV where the first part of the day is taken up with a rundown of the language associated with GV. Firstly, appropriate language and not offending clients are the main concerns for most clinicians. I also don't want the glossary to be only a purely fact-based list. As I have said previously, in my view misunderstanding and misuse of language is fundamental in working with clarity around this subject matter. As we will see during the course of the book, gaining a handle on aspects of terminology and communicating with language that is as close as possible to a common currency is how we will clear the clouds that confuse this topic and work evermore meaningfully with our GV clients.

Please note: The definitions which begin with '!' are terms that are potentially contentious, and particular care is required when encountering them. My usual rule of thumb is: 'If in doubt, ask the individual.'

AGENDER Also called genderblank, genderfree, genderless, gendervoid, non-gendered or null gender. Agender is an identity under the non-binary and transgender umbrella terms. Agender individuals find that they have no GI, although some define this more as having a gender identity that is neutral.

ANDROGYNE The combination of male and female characteristics. No one identity is more dominant than the other. This is usually expressed in fashion, gender identity, sexual identity and sexual lifestyle. Intersex is often confused with androgyny but it is very different in that androgyny is seldom used to describe an individual with the biological aspects found in intersex.

APORAGENDER From the Greek *apo/apor* ('separate' + 'gender'), this is a non-binary gender identity and umbrella term for a gender separate from male, female and anything in-between (unlike androgyne), while still having a very strong and specific gendered feeling (that is, not an absence of gender or agender). See also *Genderqueer*.

AUTOANDROPHILIA Refers to a person assigned female at birth who is sexually aroused by the thought or image of being a man. It was classified as a type of transvestic fetishism in a proposed revision to the *DSM-5* but not included in the final version. Less work has been done on autoandrophilia.

AUTOGYNEPHILIA Sexologist Ray Blanchard (1991) coined the term to describe male to female transsexuals who were sexually aroused by the idea of being women. He stated that while they lacked a specific term to describe the concept, there was evidence for the concept among clinicians of the early 20th century. Havelock Ellis (1948) used the terms 'Eonism' and 'sexo-aesthetic inversion' to describe similar cross-gender feelings and behaviours.

Today the concepts of autogynephilia and autoandrophilia (see above) are considered highly controversial amongst those who are transsexual as they are seen as essentially minimising gender dysphoria to nothing more than a sexual perversion. Blanchard's concept has long been discredited.

- ANATOMIC AUTOGYNEPHILIA Arousal to the fantasy of having a normative woman's body, or parts of one.

- BEHAVIOURAL AUTOGYNEPHILIA Arousal to the act or fantasy of doing something regarded as feminine.

- PHYSIOLOGIC AUTOGYNEPHILIA Arousal to fantasies of body functions specific to people regarded as female.

- TRANSVESTIC AUTOGYNEPHILIA Arousal to the act or fantasy of wearing typically feminine clothing.

BIGENDERED A person who feels they exhibit qualities of two genders. This may include any gender from the gender spectrum, and sometimes the individual may switch between genders (known as 'gender switching').

BINDING The act of flattening breasts by the use of constrictive materials. Common binding materials include cloth strips, elastic or non-elastic bandages, purpose-built undergarments and shirts layered from tight to loose. The act of breast binding is common for trans men but is also done by androgynous, genderqueer and gender fluid people, as well as crossdressers and performers. There can be some health risks associated with long-term binding in that it can cause deformities to the breasts and skin infections due to sweating.

BIRTH PRIVILEGE Being born into a physical body where the gender matches the subconscious gender, and the person is without question accepted as being genuine.

- CISSEXUAL PREJUDICE The belief that transsexuals' identified genders are inferior to, or less authentic than, those of cissexuals.

- CISSEXUAL PRIVILEGE Cissexual individuals consider themselves gender legitimate and unquestionable. This can be the root of transphobia.

- SOCIALISATION PRIVILEGE Being socialised into a gender which is consistent with the subconscious gender, and the person is without question accepted as being genuine.

CHOSEN GENDER Gender variant people can be very sensitive about the suggestion that they have *chosen* their gender. Professionals are recommended to talk about 'sensed gender', 'acquired gender' or 'true gender'. If in doubt, ask the individual concerned.

CISSEXUAL (AKA CIS) Where an individual's self-perception of their gender matches the sex they were assigned at birth. It is likely that the individual will have never challenged or questioned their gender identity.

CLOSETED Being aware of one's personal gender identity yet being opposed to revealing it because of various personal or social motivations. It can include denial or refusal to identify as LGBT. Overall, most reasons not to come out stem from transphobia. There are conflicts involving religious beliefs, cultural and social upbringing, and internalised transphobia, alongside feelings of fear and isolation. There are potential negative social, legal and economic consequences, such as disputes with family and peers, job discrimination, financial losses, violence, blackmail, legal actions, criminalisation, and in some countries capital punishment.

COMING OUT A figure of speech for lesbian, gay, bisexual and transgender (LGBT) people's disclosure of their sexual orientation and/or gender identity. Coming out is often framed and discussed as a privacy issue. Coming out of the closet is described and experienced as a psychological process or journey, decision-making or risk-taking; a strategy or plan; a speech act or a matter of personal identity; a rite of passage; liberation from oppression; an ordeal; and a means towards feeling trans pride instead of shame and social stigma, or even suicide.

COMMON CURRENCY Widely known and accepted.

CROSSDREAMERS A man or woman who gets aroused by the idea of being the opposite sex. Many crossdreamers identify with their birth sex, while others are gender dysphoric. Many crossdreamers understand themselves to be gender variant, while others consider themselves to be fetishists. It seems like a majority of crossdreamers are attracted to people of their own birth sex. Crossdreamers may express their feelings through crossdressing and/or creative crossdreaming (e.g. by writing stories, comics and transgender captions). Male to female crossdreamers are labelled paraphilic 'autogynephiles' in the *Diagnostic and Statistical Manual of Mental Disorders* (*DSM-5*; APA 2013), which alludes to the imaging of crossdressing for sexual arousal. Interestingly, female to male crossdreamers are not mentioned in the *DSM* at all. Some female to male crossdreamers are unhappy with this omission but most of them seem to sincerely enjoy this unexpected lack of stigmatisation. Not all crossdreamers are crossdressers.

! DEADNAME The birth name of a person (especially a transgender person) who has since changed their name, either via deed poll or statutory declaration (a cheaper and equally viable option). This can be quite a contentious topic as it is extremely insensitive to use a deadname or to refer to a deadname in relation to a gender variant person.

DEBUNKING To expose or excoriate (a claim, assertion, sentiment, etc.) as being pretentious, false or exaggerated.

DEMIGENDER From 'demi', meaning 'half' + 'gender', this is an umbrella term for non-binary gender identities that have a partial connection to a certain gender. This includes the partly female identity demigirl, and the partly male identity demiboy. There are other partial genders using the 'demi-' prefix for the same reasons (e.g. demi non-binary, demifluid, demiflux, etc.). Like non-binary, demigender is also an identity within itself, for people who feel connection to the concept of gender rather than certain genders. Being demigender is not dependent on how much (as in percentage) someone identifies as one gender; it solely depends on if a person identifies as partially. For some, they may identify with two or more genders while others may not.

DIAGNOSTIC AND STATISTICAL MANUAL OF MENTAL DISORDERS (DSM) This is an American publication published by the American Psychiatric Association (APA). The latest edition, *DSM-5* (APA 2013), stated that the term Gender Dysphoria had replaced Gender Identity Disorder. The reason given by the APA for this change was that they wanted to discourage therapists from pathologising their clients and that this was in keeping with the change in the public's view of homosexuality. (Between the years 1980 and 1987 the *DSM*'s third and fourth editions revised their classification of homosexuality and ceased regarding it as a paraphilia.)

DIY (DO-IT-YOURSELF) No, this is nothing to do with home improvement! Some individuals choose or feel compelled to self-acquire and administer their hormones, often because available doctors have too little experience in this matter, or no doctor is available in the first place. Lately, this is more to do with gender identity clinics' waiting times sometimes being in excess of 18 months for the first appointment. In some cases, the individual chooses to self-administer because their doctor will not prescribe hormones without a letter from the patient's gender specialist stating that the patient meets the criteria for a gender identity diagnosis. In these circumstances the individual may self-administer until they can get authorisations, feeling that they shouldn't have to wait for a medical professional to be convinced of their situation. However, self-administration of hormones is potentially dangerous and orally delivered hormones can cause an elevation in enzymes. To avoid this there is a requirement of regular blood-testing. Obviously, this cannot be done if the individual is self-prescribing.

DRAG This has several differing meanings depending on which sub-group you are focused on. Here I will cover the three most common:

- DRAG KING A female impersonating a male (see *Drag queen* below). May be a lesbian.

- DRAG QUEEN A male impersonating a female, often for entertainment in cabaret or social clubs. Both the clothing style and mannerisms will be exaggerated. The drag queen may be a gay man. It is worth noting that drag can be an aspect of gay Western culture.

- FAUX QUEEN/KING Another term for both of the above.

EFFEMIMANIA The cultural obsession with anything focused on male femininity. It is underpinned by traditional sexism, and the view that femininity is inferior to masculinity.

EN FEMME Crossdressing within the field of the performing arts. It has also been adopted by crossdressers to refer to when they are dressed in female attire, as opposed to 'Bob mode', which is when they are their male selves.

F2M Female to male: a gender variant man.

GAFF Something that holds a man's genitalia in place whilst crossdressed. This method uses a tube sock and the waistband from an old pair of tights or pantyhose. The outcome is to hide the penis and testicles and give a more feminine appearance. (See also *Tucking*.)

GENDER This is expressed in terms of masculinity and femininity (within our Westernised culture) and is determined and is assigned at birth, based on the sex of the individual. It affects how people perceive themselves and how they expect others to behave.

GENDER, ACQUIRED The role that a trans person achieves through the process of transition. It is the legal term in relation to the issuing of a Gender Recognition Certificate, which gives a trans person full legal rights in this gender.

GENDER, ATTRIBUTED The gender and sex that one is taken to be by others. This is usually an immediate categorisation of a person as being a man or woman, irrespective of their mode of dress.

GENDER BINARY This can mean:

- A classification system consisting of two genders: male and female.

- A concept or belief that there are only two genders and that one's biological or birth gender will align with traditional social constructs of masculine and feminine identity, expression and sexuality.

GENDER CONTINUUM A spectrum or range with which we are all aligned in some or other position. The end points of the spectrum represent female at one end and male at the other, with a mid-point which represents an equal mix of both male and female. The continuum is usually composed of five strands: biological sex, gender identity, gender expression, sexual orientation and sexual behaviour. An individual will have their own unique position for each of the strands, and the strands are not dependent on one another.

GENDER DYSPHORIA (GD) Anxiety or persistently uncomfortable feelings experienced by an individual about their assigned gender which conflicts with their internal gender identity. The Gender Recognition Panel states that gender identity disorder is 'characterised by a strong and persistent cross-gender identification' which 'does not arise from the cultural advantages of being the other sex', and it should not be confused with 'simple non-conformity to stereotypical sex role behaviour' (Gov.uk n.d.).

GENDER FLUID See *Genderqueer*.

GENDERFUCK, GENDER-BENDING, GENDER FLUID, NON-BINARY, GENDER OUTLAW The conscious effort to mock or 'fuck with' traditional notions of gender identity, gender roles and gender presentation which assumes one's identity. It challenges the common belief that an individual will assume the normative values of masculinity or femininity depending on their biological gender. Examples of people who 'genderfuck' are Annie Lennox, Boy George, Prince, Marilyn Manson and Lady Gaga.

Within the trans community there is currently a hierarchy developing where those who align more with gender fluidity see those who are M2F or F2M as following conservative values of gender binary and thus not supporting trans activism against cissexual privileges.

GENDER IDENTITY (GI) A person's perception of having a particular gender, which may or may not correspond with their birth sex.

GENDER NEUTRALITY This refers to the use of language which aims to minimise assumptions about gender or biological sex during speech. The American singer songwriter Justin Bond, who identifies as transgender, adopted the gender inclusive honorific 'Mx' to be used before his name instead of 'Mr' or 'Mrs' (i.e. Mx

Justin Bond). And personal pronoun 'v' (e.g. 'vself' instead of 'her/himself').

GENDER OUTLAW A person who defies traditional gender roles by refusing to be defined by conventional definitions of man and woman.

GENDER-POSITIVE THERAPY Having respect for, and acceptance of, people who identify somewhere on the gender spectrum at a place other than their birth sex; providing an openness to the specific needs of those as identifying with GV characteristics.

GENDERQUEER People who identify as genderqueer may think of themselves as overlapping or with blurred lines between their gender identity and sexual orientation. Being both male and female, or neither male nor female, or moving between genders (gender fluid), they will have their own name and identity for their gender.

GENDER REASSIGNMENT SURGERY (GRS) Medical term for what transsexual people often call 'gender confirmation surgery': surgery to bring the primary and secondary sex characteristics of a transsexual person's body into alignment with his or her internal perception.

GENDER RECOGNITION (GR) A process whereby a transsexual person's preferred gender is recognised in law; the achievement of the process.

- GENDER RECOGNITION ACT 2004 (GRA) The UK law which allows transsexual people to obtain gender recognition.

- GENDER RECOGNITION CERTIFICATE (GRC) A certificate which is provided to those who have been successful in their application for gender recognition. The document has no standing other than to enable the registration of births, and Department of Work and Pensions systems to be updated in line with the decision.

- GENDER RECOGNITION PANEL (GRP) A group of lawyers and doctors appointed to consider applications for gender recognition, and to approve them if the transsexual person has met the relevant criteria.

- GENDER RECOGNITION REVIEW During the early autumn of 2017, the UK Conservative government announced a review of the gender recognition process, following a national consultation. The aim was to make the process of GR easier and to de-medicalise it as many gender variant individuals claimed that the process was intrusive. There was talk of a self-declaration process to replace GR. Many non-binary individuals support this, yet I believe this was a solution to a separate topic and not a matter of reviewing the GRA (other people have raised similar concerns). The initial date at the beginning of January 2018 when the proposals were due to be announced has come and gone and at the time of writing nothing further has been heard from the review panel. It is felt by some with an interest in this matter that the government has taken on more than they expected with this review.

GENDER VARIANT (GV) Pertains to people who transcend the conventional definitions of man and woman; anyone who acts or thinks in a manner not socially approved for the gender assigned to him/her at birth. Transgendered people include pre-operative and post-operative transsexuals, transgenderists, transvestites, crossdressers, female and male impersonators, drag queens/kings, intersexuals, gender dysphorics, gender outlaws, transnaturals, variant expressives, butch lesbians, boss girls, drag queens, sissies, tomboys, transitions and everyone in-between. Some transgendered people prefer members of their own sex and some prefer members of the opposite sex; there is no correlation between gender identity and sexual orientation.

GIC An acronym for Gender Identity Clinic.

HRT (HORMONE REPLACEMENT THERAPY) For transsexual men and women HRT causes the development of many secondary sexual characteristics of their sensed gender. However, many of the existing primary and secondary sexual characteristics cannot be reversed. HRT can induce breast growth for transsexual women but not for transsexual men.

- HRT can prompt facial hair growth for transsexual men but cannot regress it for transsexual women.

- HRT may alter some characteristics such as the distribution of body fat, as well as suppress menstruation in transsexual men.

- HRT will impact the emotional experiences of the individual (e.g. oestrogen will induce a 'softer' range of emotions, and testosterone will induce a 'harder' range, such as anger).

INTERGENDER A gender identity under the non-binary and transgender umbrella. Intergender people have a gender identity that is in the middle between the binary genders of female and male and may be a mix of both. The word 'intergender' has been independently coined by different people at different times, resulting in two main differences in meaning:

- Some of them have made it into an identity label that any person can use, even if they are not intersex (dyadic). This definition seems to have been coined earlier, at least in the 1990s.

- Others have said that 'intergender' can only be used by people who are intersex, and that intergender is an identity only for intersex people. They say that intersex people need words for gender identities that correlate only with intersex bodies and that dyadic non-binary people should respect intersex people by taking up a different label than intergender for themselves, such as 'androgyne' or 'bigender'.

INTERSEX This was previously known as 'hermaphroditism'. There are more than 70 different atypical chromosomal and hormonal conditions that can cause what we would define as intersex or ambiguous genitalia. Intersexuality is something that is closer to all of us than we realise, as we will see later through the work of endocrinologist Harry Benjamin (1999). The following terms belong in this category:

- ANDROGEN INSENSITIVITY SYNDROME (AIS)
  Babies are raised as females but have an XY chromosome of a male with defective cell receptors which cause irregular development of the genitals. AIS isn't usually discovered until puberty (i.e. when the girl does not begin to menstruate). At birth the genitals appear normal, though closer inspection would reveal undescended or partially descended testes instead of ovaries, an absent uterus and cervix, and a shorter than normal vagina.

- COMPLETE ANDROGEN INSENSITIVITY SYNDROME (CAIS) AND PARTIAL ANDROGEN INSENSITIVITY SYNDROME (PAIS) This is an inherited condition which affects 1 in 20,000 individuals. It is also known as 'testicular feminisation syndrome'. In this condition the internal reproductive organs differ from the person's chromosomal profile due to a defect in their X chromosome.

- CONGENITAL ADRENAL HYPERPLASIA (CAH)
  The most prevalent cause of intersexuality amongst XX

people. It is caused by a disruption in the synthesis of cortisone while the baby is in utero. This ultimately will cause the female genitalia to appear undeveloped and masculine. The clitoris may appear ambiguous and fused to the labia or the genitalia may appear like a penis and scrotum but without the testes. The masculinisation can continue after birth. CAH can be countered with cortisone but the individual is likely to have lifelong medical issues.

- KLINEFELTER'S SYNDROME A common chromosomal condition that affects approximately 1 in 800 live male births. In this case they will have an extra X chromosome, which is inherited. Physical symptoms are smaller and firmer testes, and the ejaculate does not contain any sperm; individuals have less facial and body hair, and a smaller penis; their voice is not as deep; and they can present as less virile and are passive. Treatment involves provision of lifelong testosterone. There is controversy over whether individuals with Klinefelter's are more likely to be homosexual or transsexual, although there is no evidence to prove this.

- TURNER'S SYNDROME A chromosomal condition that occurs in approximately 1 in 2,500 female births. People with Turner's syndrome have a female body type, with non-functioning ovaries, and a lack of secondary sex characteristics unless hormone replacement is provided during late puberty. The condition can also produce other physical effects such as skeletal disorders, kidney, thyroid and hearing/ear disturbances, webbed skin and difficulties with cognitive processing.

M2F Male to female: a gender variant female.

MAVERIQUE A gender identity that falls under the non-binary umbrella. It is defined as an identity that is not the absence of gender, nor an apathy towards gender, but a present feeling of gender. This feeling of gender is completely independent from male, female or neutral, or anything derived from any of them.

MULTIGENDER An umbrella term that may also be used as a specific gender identity. Multigender identities fall under the non-binary and transgender umbrellas. The multigender umbrella includes bigender, trigender, polygender, pangender, gender fluid and possibly androgyne. Multigender individuals have more than one gender identity, either at the same time or moving between different gender identities at different times. They may or may not seek a physical transition to change their body.

NON-BINARY See *Genderqueer*.

OMNIGENDER OR POLYGENDERED Pertaining to a person whose gender identity encompasses all genders; not so much a combination of male and female, but rather the greatest common denominator of male and female.

PANGENDER A non-binary gender defined as being more than one gender. A pangender person may consider themselves a member of all genders. Pangender individuals may identify with gender inclusive or gender neutral pronouns instead of gendered ones (e.g. 'she/he' or 'her/him').

PANTOMIME DAME Female characters in a stage performance who are played by men in drag, either in extremely camp style or else by men acting butch in women's clothing. This act is not related to gay culture or sexuality, it is a parody. It is a continuation of *en travesti* (disguise), where women played males in the theatre during the 1880s. This is something which has also carried on in pantomime up to the current day with the role of 'principal boy'.

PASS Can now also mean living openly in your identified gender. It may be worth checking out what this word means to the individual.

PASSING In the context of gender, 'passing' refers to a person's ability to be regarded as a member of the sex which they physically present. Typically, passing involves a mixture of physical gender cues (e.g. hairstyle, clothing) as well as certain behavioural attributes that tend to be culturally associated with a particular gender. Irrespective of a person's presentation, many experienced dressers assert that confidence is far more important for passing than the physical aspects of appearance. Passing has also become a bit of a contentious subject, with some saying it is more important to be true to one's self than to pass in the eyes of another. This has created the question of whether people who want to pass are doing this for themselves or trying to reinforce the gender binary. The failure to 'pass' as the desired gender is referred to as 'being read'.

PHENOMENOLOGICAL METHOD This involves neither deduction nor induction to find meaning, but instead asks the researcher to intuit what is essential to the phenomenon being studied. Intuition is used to get a sense of the lived meaning of each description to relate them to what is known about the phenomenon of interest in general.

PHENOMENOLOGY This can mean the science of phenomena as distinct from that of the nature of being; an approach that concentrates on the study of consciousness and the objects of direct experience.

PHENOMENON This can mean:

- Anything that can be perceived as an occurrence or fact by the senses.

- Any remarkable occurrence or person.

- In philosophy, it can be the object of perception, experience, etc., or (in the writings of Kant) a thing as it appears and is interpreted in perception and reflection, as distinguished from its real nature as a thing-in-itself.

PINAFORING OR PETTICOATING A type of forced feminisation that involves dressing a man or boy in girls' clothing. While the practice has come to be a rare, socially unacceptable form of humiliating punishment, it has risen up as a subgenre of erotic literature or other expression of sexual fantasy.

PRE-OP/POST-OP Pre-operative and post-operative; having had or not had gender confirmation surgeries. Pre-operative implies that the person desires gender corrective surgery.

- NON-OP A person who does not desire surgery or does not need surgery to feel comfortable in his or her body.

SEX The physical body: male or female.

! SEX CHANGE, TRANNY, 'THE CHOP' These terms still appear in the media from time to time and are regarded as offensive and inaccurate. Note that some gender variant people are beginning to 'reclaim' the word 'tranny' in much the same way that lesbian and gay people have reclaimed 'queer'. This is not recommended for anyone who is not a member of those communities.

SEX REASSIGNMENT SURGERY (SRS) Also known as 'gender reassignment surgery', 'gender confirmation surgery', 'genital reconstruction surgery', 'gender-affirming surgery' and 'sex re-alignment surgery'. It is the surgical procedure (or procedures) by which a gender variant person's physical appearance and function of their existing sexual characteristics are altered to resemble that socially associated with their identified gender. It can be part of a treatment for gender dysphoria in transgender people. Related genital surgeries may also be performed on intersex people, often in infancy.

SEXUALITY Who we are sexually attracted to. This can include any permutation (i.e. heterosexual, homosexual, bisexual, polysexual, asexual, or any other version of erotic attraction).

! SHEMALE (SHE-MALE) A term used primarily (but not exclusively) in sex work to describe a transsexual woman who has undertaken hormone therapy and has augmented breasts; however, it is likely she will have a penis. Using the term 'shemale' to describe a transsexual woman is considered highly offensive, for it suggests she works in the sex industry. It is often regarded as a derogatory term and should never be used.

SISSY OR SISSIFICATION In the BDSM practice of forced feminisation, the male bottom undergoing crossdressing may be called a sissy as a form of erotic humiliation, which may elicit guilt or sexual arousal, or possibly both, depending on the individual.

STANDARDS OF CARE (SOC) The guidelines provided by the NHS, and taken from WPATH, which oversee and direct the means by which gender variant individuals receive care and treatment. The overall goal of the SOC is: 'To provide clinical guidance for health professionals to assist transgender, transsexuals, and gender non-conforming people with safe and effective pathways to lasting personal comfort with their gendered selves, in order to maximise their overall health, psychological well-being, and self-fulfillment' (WPATH 2012).

STEALTH Having transitioned to your sensed gender, then living where nobody in your current life knows your previous gender history or sees you as anyone other than who you are. In some extreme cases individuals have chosen to remove everyone from their life who knew them in their previous gender role. Much like passing, this is another contentious topic.

! TERF (TRANS-EXCLUSIONARY RADICAL FEMINIST) A group of feminists who claim that trans women aren't really women, as biological determinism is only a fallacy when it is used against them, not when they use it against others.

TRANSGENDER/TRANS See *Gender variant*.

TRANSGENDER HATE CRIME When a transphobic hate incident becomes a criminal offence, it's known as a hate crime. There are no specific transphobic hate crimes. Any criminal offence can be a hate crime if the offender targeted you because of their prejudice or hostility against LGBT people. When someone is charged with a transphobic hate crime, the judge can impose a tougher sentence on the offender under the Criminal Justice Act 2003.

TRANSITION The social, psychological, emotional and economic processes that a gender variant person undergoes to move from their assigned gender role into their sensed or acquired gender. The time this takes is variable and depends on the individual's ability to embrace significant change in their life. If requiring genital surgery, the individual will have to undergo a so-called 'Real Life Test' (i.e. living in the acquired gender role for a minimum of one year).

TRANSPHOBIA Dislike of or prejudice against transsexual, gender variant or transgender people.

TRANSSEXUAL A condition where an individual identifies with a gender inconsistent or not culturally associated with their assigned sex. A medical diagnosis can be made (gender dysphoria) if the person experiences discomfort due to the dysphoria. They may wish to choose to undergo sex reassignment surgery.

! TRANSSEXUAL This should not be used as a noun ('a transsexual'). It is best used as an adjective to qualify other descriptive characteristics (i.e. 'transsexual people'; 'trans people'; 'transsexual woman'; 'trans woman'). Otherwise, it is similar to referring to someone as 'a black' or 'a disabled'. Note that some trans people prefer to be described as 'women' or 'men'. *Note:* Please consider the entry *Gender variant* when using the term 'transgender'.

TRANSVESTITE/CROSSDRESSING The act of wearing clothing commonly associated with the opposite sex within that respective society. The individual concerned may adopt feminine behaviour or traits. This does not however indicate a transsexual identity and as such does not mean the person is seeking hormones or surgery. In the late 19th and early 20th centuries the term 'transvestism' was interchangeable with 'homosexuality' (or 'inverts' as they were also called).

TRIGENDER A non-binary identity in which one shifts among three genders, which could include male, female and a non-binary gender. Someone who is also genderqueer may mix two or more genders at a time. Trigender falls under the general category of genderqueer or androgyny, a gender identity that goes beyond the normal binary gender system (male and female) and tends to be a catch-all place for other gender identities. It can also be seen as a culture that recognises how individuals can define their own sense of self. See also *Genderqueer*.

TUCKING Tucking is the practice, well known in both gender variant and drag circles, of putting one's penis between and behind one's legs, so that it's not visible from the front of the body. Some people push their testicles back as well, while others move them upward and rest them on the lower part of their abdomen before securing them in place. There are a number of reasons why gender variant women tuck: both for their own sense of self, and to influence how others perceive them. For people who experience gender dysphoria related to the appearance of their body, it's a way for them to feel like their body matches the gender they feel inside. There are some health concerns with this process because when the testicles are tucked inside the body they can be prone to overheating, which can lead to fertility issues. The process of tucking by using either tape or a gaff means that it is impossible to urinate. This means that individuals will avoid drinking, which can lead to dehydration. Also, because the tucking creates warm and hot parts of the body, there is a risk of skin infections. See also *Gaff*.

WPATH (WORLD PROFESSIONAL ASSOCIATION FOR TRANSGENDER HEALTH) Formerly known as the 'Harry Benjamin International Gender Dysphoria Association' (HBIGDA), this is a professional organisation devoted to the understanding and treatment of gender identity disorders.

WPATH STANDARDS OF CARE (SOC) The objective of the WPATH *Standards of Care* is to provide clinical guidance for medical professionals to assist transsexual, transgender and gender non-conforming people with safe and effective pathways to achieving lasting personal comfort with their gendered selves, in order to maximise their overall health, psychological well-being and self-fulfilment. This assistance may include primary care, gynaecological and urological care, reproductive options, voice and communication therapy, mental health services (e.g. assessment, counselling, psychotherapy), and hormonal and surgical treatments.

CHAPTER 1

THIS DIVERSE PLANET

Biodiversity versus Gender Bigotry

When I began planning the purpose of Part 1, I felt it was incredibly important to try to unravel what the years of training in the field of GI have shown me: namely that even with therapists there is a lot of confusion around what GI is. What has concerned me is that these counsellors and therapists have rarely explored or examined their own GI within their initial professional training. This is something which I believe needs addressing and changing if we as professionals are to lead from the front and bring about positive and fundamental change in how we view GI.

If we consider that counsellors and therapists have a limited grasp of GI – and we are supposed to have done 'work on ourselves' within our training and personal therapy as we develop that all-important self-awareness – then is it any surprise that those outside this profession have even less of a grasp of what GI is?

This makes it clearer why here in the West we have such a limited relationship with our GI. The main complexity we face is confusion and misunderstanding about what we are engaging with. A very simple and clear example of this is GI's inclusion within the acronym of LGBT. It sometimes feels like this acronym is a receptacle for depositing all those who do not identify as Western binary gender heterosexuals!

The 'T' stands for 'transgender' in LGBT and, as we know, this represents GI. It focuses on how you feel about yourself, and which gender you sense yourself to be; lesbian, gay and bisexual, on the other hand, are all focused around sexual attraction/preference and erotic love. As a 'trans' person I would prefer the 'T' not to be included because to most people, who don't give it much consideration, it causes confusion. Whilst I recognise that those who make up the 'L', 'G' and 'B' have had to make sense of their sexuality whilst facing difficulties, hatred and prejudice, still their concerns are very different from those of people under the trans umbrella. What complicates the subject further is that these are matters which affect us ALL. Yes, every one of us.

So, let's be clear what we are working with. What are the factors at play within each one of us? Figure 1 illustrates this and helps us to understand the complexity. As we separate gender and sexuality into their individual components, we can view each aspect in its true form. Each strand is complete and clarifies what so often gets confused and misunderstood when considering gender and sexuality. Figure 1 applies to everyone. We are all doing each thread of this composition in our own unique way even if we don't think we are and consider ourselves unremarkable. Even biological sex will be individual as no two men or women's chromosomes and hormones will be an exact match, even if they consider themselves to be a biological man or woman.

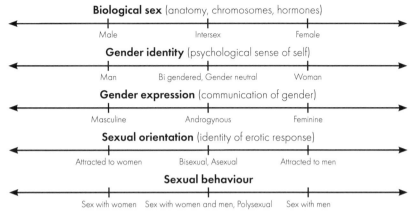

FIGURE 1: GENDER AND SEXUALITY

Among the 7.5 billion people inhabiting the planet Earth we will all be exceptional in our biological composition, GI and sexual orientation. We are more diverse and unique than we possibly perceive ourselves to be. We find that our GI really is our own if we begin to look at the subtleties of it. We should now begin to consider the bigger picture of how this sits with other species on Earth.

Living in this modern society, many of us can feel that we humans are very different, and possibly far more developed from other species. We have made advances in technologies and in our ability to think and communicate with one another on the many platforms that are available to us. However, while these developments are important in their respective fields, they are merely filters which stand to distance us from ourselves and the subtleties of being human. 'So, who are we then?' Well, we are one of the 8.7 million species living on Earth at the last count in 2011. We are governed by the same laws that affect all other forms of life and, ultimately, we are formed of the same chemical and biological compounds as other species.

Problems arise from our complexity as a species. We are paradoxical in that we have conscious thought and an ability to question ourselves and our existence. We can engage in a multitude of activities, including the arts, philosophy, theology, faith practices, sciences and travel. We try to understand our emotional world and connect to one another through various forms of communication. However, we are fundamentally simplistic in that we excrete, sustain our life force via nourishment, become emotionally attached to others, have the capacity to love and be loved, have sex for pleasure, can reproduce, can hurt and be hurt emotionally and physically, put substances into our bodies to feel different, become susceptible to illnesses, bleed and break, and ultimately all die. What appears to cause us difficulties in accepting the more simplistic aspects of ourselves – the being a human and 'being-in-the-world' (a phrase coined by German philosopher and seminal thinker Martin Heidegger) – is the interplay between these two polarities of complex and simple. Here lies the problem, as Ernesto Spinelli discusses in his book *The Interpreted World*:

> For Heidegger, a human being is a *Dasein* which, literally translated, means "being there," which has been more commonly translated into English as being-in-the-world. This position holds that, not only are we unique (as far as we know today) in our ability to be aware of our existence, but this awareness reveals an inseparable relationship between existence and the world. Our awareness is not solely subjective, but rather, intersubjective. (Spinelli 1989, p.108)

The history of humankind is littered with examples of these complexities at play. Religion, politics and economic and civil laws all place pressures through social rules that shape and maintain what is the desired socially acceptable order of things. To be outside any given order, as we are beginning to see, is to put oneself in a very vulnerable place which could lead in the worst-case scenario to eradication by those within the acceptable order.

An example of the interplay between these polarities can be found in the works of the naturalist Charles Darwin. We still acknowledge and regard his work as having played a significant part of how we understand the natural world. However, his works are merely a stepping stone in the study of the evolution of various species. We are still influenced heavily by Darwinian theory, even with evidence mounting towards a contrary view. His theory of 'natural selection' appears to be largely still accepted (Darwin 1809), although the overarching belief that nature is selfish and protective, and the idea of a 'red in tooth-and-claw struggle' for existence, has been dropped to allow for a less selfish version of nature. When it comes to his theory of 'sexual selection', there is no explanation about gender multiplicity, which he was aware of as he had already conducted studies on barnacles and understood that they had both male and female sex organs. This was simply ignored. There is every likelihood that there was a patriarchal subversion of silence to ensure his theory went unchallenged for decades. This continued right up until recent history, as evolutionary biologist Joan Roughgarden discovered for herself when she challenged and addressed Darwin's failings in her controversial book *Evolution's Rainbow: Diversity, Gender, and Sexuality in Nature and People* (2004). Some biologists had already come to acknowledge gender diversity within nature, but it was regarded as the exception.

Initially, Roughgarden was criticised for suggesting the concept of gender multiplicity. However, the reality is hard to ignore with the breadth of current evidence pointing towards diversity amongst many species on this planet. Darwin's theory is inadequate as it again fails to address the variations of bodies, behaviours and life histories that exist.

It feels like we humans have raised ourselves up and in doing so have distanced ourselves from other life forms by not applying the same rules of nature to ourselves. This is especially true when it comes to sexuality and gender.

A study which took place in 1999 determined that there are around 1,500 species displaying gender multiplicity within the animal kingdom. This is far more than what we normally believe to be the case, as stated by the Canadian biologist Bruce Bagemihl, author of the study:

> The traditional view of the animal kingdom – what we might call the Noah's ark view – is that biology revolves around two sexes, male and female, with one of each pair. The range of genders and sexualities actually found in the animal world, however, is considerably richer than this. Animals with females that become males, animals with no males at all, animals that are both male and female simultaneously, animals where males resemble females, animals where females court other females and males who are the males – Noah's ark was never quite like this! (Bagemihl 1999, p.36)

When considering gender multiplicity Joan Roughgarden states: 'All species have genetic diversity – their biological rainbow. No exceptions. Biological rainbows are universal and eternal. Yet biological rainbows have posed difficulties for biologists since the beginning is of evolutionary theory' (Roughgarden 2004, p.13).

To clarify, there are species which display transvestic traits (i.e. they visually change sex) and there are species which display transvestic behaviours (i.e. they do things which we would typically assume to be associated with the opposite sex). And there are some species which display transsexual traits (i.e. they physically change sex). Let's look at some examples:

- Female African swallowtail butterflies look like males in their colour and patterning.

- Female musk-oxen have a patch of hair on their forehead which mimics the male's hornshield.

- Female Chinese water deer have grown tufts of hair on either side of their jaw which resemble the tusks of the male.

- Shrimps, oysters and woodlice will all undertake a sex change at some point in their life. (Interestingly, Darwin was aware of the barnacle's hermaphroditic status (the presentation of both male and female reproductive organs) but struggled to fit this into his theory of sexual selection!)

- Cuttlefish appear to change sex by changing their exterior colours to those of the opposite sex, a form of transvestic appearance if you will.

- Clown fish (Nemo, in Disney's *Finding Nemo*, is a clown fish) have a floating gender presentation – what we would call 'gender fluid' in humans.

- Female spotted hyenas can enlarge their clitoris to make it look like a penis.

- In many shark species the female can reproduce without a male.

- Female seahorses never bear the young – this is accomplished by the male.

- White-throated sparrows have two types of males and two types of females.

- The real masters/mistresses of gender flexibility are known as 'bidirectional sex changers' and are found among parrot fish, wrasses, groupers and angelfish. During their lifetime they undergo a complete sex reversal. Females become males, functioning ovaries become functioning testes, and the fish are still able to reproduce in their changed form.

- Then there are what biologists refer to as 'hermaphrodites'. These are species (there are around 65,000 of them) where the organism (animal, fish, etc.) has reproductive organs normally associated with both male and female sexes. Many groups of animals (particularly invertebrates) do not have separate sexes. For these groups, hermaphroditism is considered a normal condition, enabling a form of sexual reproduction in which either partner can act as the 'female' or 'male'. Examples include the hamlet fish, sea bass, some slugs and snails, earthworms and mangrove killifish, to name but a few.

- And just so I'm not leaving plants out of the frame, the paw paw has 31 sexes, whilst most plants can be considered hermaphrodites because they make pollen and seeds simultaneously (pollen is the male part of the plant and the ovule part of the seed is the female part).

As you can see, there is a wealth of diversity going on within other Earth species, which leads me to think that diversity of presentation is natural. This therefore poses the question of whether gender and sexual diversity are also *'natural'*; in other words, if such diversity naturally manifests in many other 'Earth species', what makes *us* (the human species) believe that we are above it applying to us as well? Not accepting that the human species follows this same evolutionary development places our species in the shadows, a freak of nature surrounded by these seemingly less advanced creatures!

The word 'hermaphroditism' was used in the past to describe any person whose physical sex characteristics did not precisely fit male or female classifications. However, the term has been replaced by 'intersex'. Intersex describes a wide variety of combinations of what are considered male and female biology. Intersex biology may include, for example, ambiguous-looking external genitalia. As mentioned previously, the endocrinologist Harry Benjamin (1999) said we are all a bit intersex in regard to our chromosomes and the details of our biological make-up. This beautiful quote from the website of the UK Intersex Association illustrates the delicate nature of our biological composition, and the balance that exists between the variety within our species and the futility of trying to define normality:

But the complexity and possibilities of variation are what guarantee that each of us is a unique individual. Nature does not create clones and each of us is the only one of us there ever has been, is, or ever will be. Therefore, trying to apply terms like 'normal' to human beings is quite absurd. You are the only you there has ever been or ever will be, therefore you are the perfectly normal you. When everything is different and unique, then everything is normal. (Hayes-Light 2017)

It is commonly accepted that, chromosomally, a female is XX and a male is XY. However, nature being nature, this formation doesn't always occur. Each human usually has a set of 23 pairs of chromosomes in each cell of their body. The initial 22 pairs are called 'autosomes' and the 23rd pair are known as 'sex chromosomes'. The way of distinguishing the formation of the chromosomes is by 'karyotype'. Someone with a 23rd pair of chromosomes which are both X chromosomes will be identified as karyotype '46, XX'. This tells us that they have the usual 46 chromosomes (23 pairs) and that the 23rd pair ('sex chromosomes') are both X chromosomes. Someone with a 23rd pair of chromosomes consisting of one X and one Y will be identified as karyotype '46, XY'. Many people are born with more or fewer sex chromosomes than the typical simple pair. They may have three sex chromosomes (e.g. two X and one Y, in which case they will be identified as karyotype '47, XXY'). Alternatively, they may have only one sex chromosome, an X, in which case they will be identified as karyotype '45, X0'.

The medical services cause controversy by describing those intersex people as having 'disorders of sex development or DSD' (Hayes-Light 2017). Dr Jay Hayes-Light, Director of the UK Intersex Association, said of this matter: 'The term "DSD" was, of course, not devised by intersex people, but by a group of non-elected mainly science males who (whatever they may say) were becoming worried that medicine was losing its grip on what happens to intersex people. So, they meet and re-pathologise a natural variation' (Hayes-Light 2017).

The term 'DSD' is robustly contested by those experiencing the condition and support services. I believe there is something deeply unhelpful about using language that is judgemental.

Inthecase of DSD, what does 'disorder' imply about an individual with this diagnosis? That they are damaged in their development, that they are not normal...and by whose standards? And while I'm not intersex, I have shared a similar experience to this in the language used to describe those who are GV. The American Psychological Association's *Diagnostic and Statistical Manual* (*DSM*) only changed 'Gender Identity Disorder' to 'Gender Dysphoria' in the 2013 edition (*DSM-5*). This late change will not have helped the many trans people who have had to manage bigotry and poor treatment from gender services over the years. The other thing to say in relation to gender dysphoria featuring in this mental health classification manual is that I have never considered myself to be experiencing a mental health condition because my GI doesn't fall within the narrow band width of the binary...but more on that later. Dare I say that it could be mentally frail not to question who you are and rely on the designation given at birth? But I wouldn't dream of saying such a thing!

As is now evidenced, we have people who present as intersex, and GV can be represented as a branch of the tree which is the human species. As humans are a branch of the evolutionary tree which includes all Earth's species, a healthy approach is to regard intersex and transgender as examples of human diversity that are legitimate manifestations within nature. Remember, evolutionary scientists now recognise that gender multiplicity in other species is normal and natural, so why should we consider ourselves to be any different?

Why should people who are intersex or trans experience difficulties, pain and suffering (as I myself have done)? Being cissexual (being comfortable with one's birth sex) shouldn't be regarded as an all-encompassing truth of how humans are meant to be.

Within our species variation, poor understanding, assumptions and fear are fertile soil for hatred to germinate and flourish in. This is where hatred begins, and it can become transphobia and even transphobic hate crime. These are terms we have seen evolve within the last few years, yet the behaviours which have led to these terms coming into existence have been around for centuries. As we shall explore in the next chapter, trans is not a recent phenomenon and versions of it go far back in history over many continents and cultures. We will explore why we in the West appear to have such a limited vocabulary in relation to doing GI, while yet seemingly less-developed cultures around the world have always had not only a richer GI vocabulary but also a healthier comprehension and recognition of the many ways that we as a species can 'do' gender – that is, until Western civilisation had its say.

CHAPTER 2

HISTORICAL MISINTERPRETATIONS, POWER SHIFTS AND GENDER SUPPRESSION

One of the standard arguments that gets hauled out by conservative Christians when the question of whether GV people are legitimate in the eyes of God is this quote from Deuteronomy: 'A woman shall not wear man's clothing, nor shall a man put on a woman's clothing; for whoever does these things is an abomination to the Lord your God' (Deuteronomy 22:5).

Firstly, to be clear, this quote comes from Mosaic Law – the Law of Moses (i.e. Hebrew and Jewish), so it may not necessarily be applied to those outside of the Jewish faith. It is also important to note that, at the time the Bible was written, GV as we know it today didn't exist. If you read the Bible you won't find words such as 'crossdressing', 'transsexualism' or 'gender fluidity', because these phenomena didn't occur as we recognise them now.

I do so want to clarify that trans people weren't a unique phenomenon at the time of the early Christians. There are cultures and societies all over the planet that had, and still do have, expressions of GV; but sticking with the Christian dimension for a moment, let's look at this quote from Jesus to get a flavour for how GV might have been regarded:

> For there are eunuchs who have been so from birth, and there are eunuchs who have been made eunuchs by men, and there are eunuchs who have made themselves eunuchs for the sake of the kingdom of heaven. Let the one who is able to receive this receive it. (Matthew 19:12)

The eunuchs (castrated males) that Jesus was referring to appear to have been perceived as belonging in several categories: those made by others, those made by their own hand and those who were eunuchs from birth, whom Jews called '*saris chamah*' or 'eunuchs of the sun' (i.e. those who were known to be eunuchs from the day the sun first shone upon them). 'Eunuchs of the sun' appears to be a reference to what we regard as intersex today. Jews took this status of sun eunuchs seriously and made provisions for these naturally born eunuchs in their communities – borrowing from laws for men and laws for women to make sure all their bases were covered.

And then there are these quotes from Genesis about evolution:

> The LORD God made all kinds of trees grow out of the ground – trees that were pleasing to the eye and good for food. (Genesis 2:9)

> Now the LORD God had formed out of the ground all the wild animals and all the birds in the air: and brought them unto Adam to see what he would name them: and whatsoever Adam called each living creature, that was the name thereof. (Genesis 2:19)

So here we have two clear quotes of God creating the animals of planet Earth. And as we now know from the previous chapter, we have a wealth of gender multiplicity within animal species, so it must be assumed from the two quotes that it was God's choice to make animals the way that we find them.

When we study theological texts by modern-day theological explorers it becomes clear are that there was, and still is, confusion around what is gender-related and what is sexual activity-related. And as I've noted earlier, the inclusion of the 'T' within LGBT continues to cause even greater confusion between what is sexual behaviour and what is related to GI. This may appear like a very simple point; however, it is a simple point which has ramifications for trans people trying to live their lives. When radical conservative Christians attack the LGBT population, we can now see they have a confused argument if we consider Matthew 19:12. The rest of the Christian faith would appear to be accepting of GV, with there being several ordained priests and clergy around the world who would be considered GV.

The trouble with the meaning within religious texts is that something gets lost in the interpretation; they can be interpreted in any way the reader chooses to suit their personal needs or agendas. It can be like the game 'Chinese Whispers' where a message is passed between several people and the message that arrives at the end is usually changed by being misheard as it's passed between the players. If we sweep away the interpretations of the millennia and look at the text again with fresh eyes, as we have done with Deuteronomy 22:5 and Matthew 19:12, we can begin to see a very different intent in the passages. Let's try this process again but with the Quran. What does *it* say about GV?

> To Allah belongs the dominion of the heavens and the earth; He creates what he wills. He gives to whom He wills female [children], and He gives to whom He wills males. (Quran, 42:49)

> He makes them [both] males and females, and He renders whom He wills barren. Indeed, He is Knowing and Competent. (Quran, 42:50)

The verses in fact describe varieties of gender – Allah clearly says that He makes them BOTH male and female. The verses can refer to physical, psychological or both forms of ambiguity; if Allah wishes it, so be it.

And then there is this:

> And it is He who spread the earth and placed therein firmly set mountains and rivers; and from all the fruits He made therein two mates; He causes the night to cover the day. Indeed, in that are signs for a people who give thought. (Quran, 13:3)

Here the Quran refers to every kind of fruit being made in pairs: male and female. And from the verses in the 42nd chapter (quoted above), we can conclude that there is gender ambiguity in plants as well. Why? ...Because plants, as we know from the previous chapter, can present in gender multiplicities. The scripture quotations presented here are taken directly from the Quran, but they are also described in the *Hadith* (which are accepted prophetic traditions), therefore we know there are various representations of Allah's will.

As we saw with Christianity, versions of GV are evidenced by the existence of eunuchs. Islam also had GV within its culture. Mukhannathun were an identifiable group of men who publicly adopted feminine adornments such as clothing and jewellery. Again, they were described in the *Hadith*, so we know they were an accepted part of Islamic culture.

Mukhannathaun appeared to be quite varied in their presentation, as well as in their roles within Islamic society. Their blend of male and female enabled them to traverse the borders of the sexes. They acted as chaperones, as due to their combined GI they were considered to have a licence to be with women, and to be matchmakers (for eligible bachelors), musicians, entertainers and advisers to those in authority. They were known to have relationships predominantly with women, although there are accounts of some Mukhannathun engaging in relationships with men (it is worth noting that homosexuality is condemned in the Quran). There is an account of one such Mukhannathun, named Al-Dalal, who inappropriately propositioned a couple whose marriage he had arranged. On their wedding night, he engaged in sexual relations with both of them. The ruler at the time, Sulayman, was outraged on learning about this and ordered the punishment that all Mukhannathun be castrated. Interestingly, this punishment wasn't for the presentation of homosexuality but rather for the corruption of a woman. So, we again see more confusion around sexuality and gender.

As we have seen, gender within both Christianity and Islam isn't cut and dried. It would be beneficial to look next at how Judaism regards GI.

Abrahamic religions have creation stories in which God creates people, male and female. This is sometimes interpreted as a divine command against GV. The Torah contains specific exclusions on crossdressing and the damaging of genitals. However, as you may now be beginning to realise, what constitutes gender and what is permissible regarding its presentation is not so clear – it depends on which strand of the faith you are looking at.

Within Judaism the term *saris* (used to denote what we would call 'eunuchs' or 'chamberlains') appears 45 times in the Tanakh (also referred to as the Mikra or Hebrew Bible). Overall, *saris* were an accepted part of society and religious law.

Orthodox Judaism proclaims that sex/gender is innate and eternal based on verses in the Book of Genesis about Adam and Eve and the creation of maleness and femaleness. Sex-change operations involving the removal of genital organs are forbidden. Yet paradoxically, Orthodox authorities recognise the efficacy of sex reassignment surgery (SRS) in changing *halachic* (collective Jewish laws) sex designation.

Hasidic Judaism has no place for trans people as everything in the community is determined by gender roles. Most Hasidic Jews are barely aware of trans people, and the topic is never discussed.

The first person to come out as trans in a Hasidic community was trans activist and writer Abby Stein. When she came out she was shunned by her family and the Hasidic community. Conservative Judaism has mixed views on transgender people. In 2003 the Committee on Jewish Law and Standards approved a rabbinic ruling that established that SRS is permissible as a treatment of gender dysphoria, and that a transgender person's sex status under Jewish law is changed by SRS. However, there have not been any open trans rabbis or trainee rabbis.

Reconstructionist Judaism has expressed positive views on transgender people, and a resolution committing themselves to work for full inclusion, acceptance, appreciation, celebration and welcome of people of all gender identities in Jewish life has been approved.

Reform Judaism has expressed positive views on transgender people. The following examples acknowledge that the ancestors of the faith were quite progressive in their outlook on gender.

- **Zachar:** This term is derived from the word for a pointy sword, and can be regarded as a phallus.

- **Nekeivah:** This term is derived from the word for a crevice and is likely to be referring to a vagina.

- **Androgynos:** A person who has both 'male' and 'female' sexual characteristics.

- **Tumtum:** A person whose sexual characteristics are indeterminate or obscured.

- **Ay'lonit:** A person who is identified as 'female' at birth but develops 'male' characteristics at puberty and is infertile.

- **Saris:** A person who is identified as 'male' at birth but develops 'female' characteristics at puberty and/or is lacking a penis. Saris can be 'naturally' saris (saris hamah) or become one through human intervention.

(Medwed 2015)

I think what has been indicated so far by considering other religions is that it's simply impossible to understand what one or two verses might mean without looking at them in the entire context of culture, time, related writings, and where they appear. Therefore, when radicals and fundamentalists from any religion do this, they look foolish for claiming that they can.

Within the LGBT initialism 'T' stands for 'transgender' and is really an anomaly as it's gender-focused, not sexuality-focused. The Bible, the Quran and the Torah are quite clear in their views about homosexuality; however, as we have seen, their position is less confused when considering GV. And yet, there are large parts of the population who are confused and see sexuality and gender as the same thing. As mentioned previously, I'm wondering whether the LGBT acronym should change and maybe the 'T' should now make its own way in the world.

We understand that GV is not a new concept – it was experienced by ancient cultures very differently and referred to by different terms. But what is fundamentally at its core is the same (i.e. varying expressions of GI). So, what has been happening between those ancient times and the current surge of interest which began in 2014? Well, the late trans activist Leslie Feinberg has written a comprehensive and passionate history about the various expressions of gender multiplicity throughout many worldwide cultures in his book *Transgender Warriors* (1996).

Our earliest ancestors do not appear to have been biological determinists. There are societies all over the world that allowed for more than two sexes, as well as respecting the right of the individuals to reassign their sex. Transsexuality, transgender, intersexuality and bigendered appear as themes in creation stories, legends, parables and oral histories (Feinberg 1996).

It is important for us as counsellors and therapists that we begin to support GV presentations in history in a way that has not been fully comprehended previously. And for us to be able to do this we need to understand what happened in the development of our society, so we can make sense of why these societies have come to have such an uncomfortable relationship with GV. For us to be able to do this we need to take a look at the bigger picture and to take a slight historical diversion and time travel back to 4,000 BCE. By looking at how societies we are familiar with came into being, we will see how the ruling few determined for the many what was and wasn't acceptable culturally, societally and, more importantly, personally.

The Dominant View of Societal Evolution (or at Least the Story We Are Told)

It is not within the scope of this book to survey the sociological and cultural implications of how the evolution of humanity as a species evolved from hunter-gatherers into the post-agricultural modern era. However, there were social and cultural repercussions within this evolution. There were untruths constructed by the powerful few as a means of domination and subjugation of the many who made up society, and as a result the human species would never be the same again. It is these untruths that I'm interested in, both in terms of the undertaking of this book and how we as people can begin to claim back some of our own truth. So, allow me to place things into a wider context around what happened during the evolution of humanity, beginning with the time we call 'pre-civilisation' or 'prehistory'. This was the time of our hunter-gatherer ancestors (also referred to as cavemen). The common view is that these early civilisations were violent, cannibalistic and savage. We can assume that these cultures continued to exist in pockets throughout the world, that it was considered they needed 'civilising' and that the role of 'civilised society' was to save them from themselves. This way of thinking has been used as justification for waging wars on other cultures for thousands of years. The British academic Steve Taylor challenges this widely held view in his book *The Fall* (2005). He gives a very different view of prehistory, beginning with the lives of the hunter-gatherer tribes through to 4,000 BCE.

It is the period 11,000–4,000 BCE, commonly known as the Neolithic era, which sees the beginning of the transition in the social and physical landscape with the development of agriculture, which rapidly expands and ultimately replaces hunter gathering. During this transition, people begin moving into settlements of varying sizes; however, with this transition there is also a loss in the quality of the social structure. According to Taylor, it appears that the hunter-gatherers were living in societies which were relatively non-hierarchical. Burial sites of this time seem to show that there was no inequality of status; there is evidence of gender role differentiation, but there also appears to be mutual respect between the sexes. It would also appear there was little to no evidence of either patriarchy or matriarchy and these cultures appeared to be egalitarian. Within these societies the elderly, disabled and infirm were taken care of and differences between people, regardless of who they were, were not considered an issue. Decisions that affected the overall group, although ultimately made by the chief or elder, were only made once everyone had had a chance to speak and be heard. It appears that the people of this time lived in relatively equal cultures with a fairer distribution of wealth and much less inequality than we are used to. It would also appear that there were gender role differences; however, there is evidence of both men and women being buried with equal attention. These people lived in more peaceful times. It is only with the so-called evolution and modernisation of society that these ways of being were changed to the structure we are more familiar with.

Around 4,000 BCE, we begin to see big changes not only with the first cities and people moving *en masse* to live within them; it was also at this time the world entered a period of rapid global warming, with temperatures rising significantly in the space of a few hundred years. This would have had a knock-on effect with overwhelming crop failures and people facing starvation. To survive, people had to organise themselves by protecting what they had. In some cases, survival meant being prepared to raid your neighbour's resources. Cities became city-states, along with expansionist ideas aimed at neighbouring cities and safeguarding survival. This led to aggression and hostility and the need for self-protection. Thus, organised armies came into being and these were controlled by warlords. The world was becoming a violent place. We see the loss of an egalitarian society and the rise of inequality as one group of society appropriated power and oppressed another. An example of this was men taking power from women and patriarchy being born. With power came wealth, and the emergence of an age of kings and rulers, empires and emperors with vast riches, yet there were many within the population who were left to starve. Gone were the times when societies cared for all their members. Societies had moved from a 'leaver culture' of the hunter-gatherers, where they only took what they needed as a means of survival, to a 'taker culture' where the aim became to amass surplus with no regard for animals or other species. This is still where humanity is firmly embedded.

These early modern societies may have looked very different to the society we live in now, yet they are the origins which lead up to our current place on the timeline of humanity. Here in the West we are all consequences of that fall. Everything we have today – social structure, laws, religion, scientific advances (including technology) – all come from that. And with so much technology, healthcare and food options at our disposal, how can we regard the fall as anything but beneficial? We may think how lucky we are to have all this at our disposal as well as freedom in our modern society; yet we also have inequality, intolerance and hatred of difference, poor and inappropriate distribution of wealth, laws that are determined through fear to keep the few safe and the many vulnerable, and finally, in reality, a lack of freedom – these, too, are products of the fall.

We may think we are free in our Western societies to really be who we believe ourselves to be, but I can tell you as a GV woman that we are not free. I am not free to always hold my wife's hand in public if I wish to do so, through consideration that this simple and loving act might offend or engender disgust and hatred in a casual onlooker and thus bring about some vile act of hostility upon us. This is the conditioning that we have all been exposed to by the civilisations we now live in and they are products of the fall. Therefore, I believe that GI is one of the last battlegrounds for a real freedom which implicates us all, but more of this later.

Steve Taylor noted that it is during the time of the fall and the rise of city-states, which became governed by warlords and then by kings or emperors, that we see the emergence of formalised religions with gods and goddesses. However, these weren't benevolent gods. They interfered in the lives of men and women, and they exhibited ugly and merciless behaviours requiring sacrifices from their followers to ensure favourable outcomes, yet demanding to be worshipped and followed. These so-called gods were the manifestations of the people who had taken control and established the modern societies, and to ensure they maintained control over their people they exerted power through demands and fear. These deities became extensions of themselves, if not reinventions of themselves, and demanded absolute devotion and commitment in return for safety. Remarkably, these early gods were not as restrictive as we see them become in later centuries. The likes of Ashtoreth, Ishtar, Isis and Cybele are interestingly reoccurring figures that were worshipped by many different societies over a wide geographic region for millennia, including people in the Bronze Age, those in Classical Antiquity, the Canaanites and the Phoenicians. Some of these goddesses were taken on as cult heads in Egyptian, Roman, Mesopotamian, Assyrian, Ancient Greek and Babylonian societies.

For these religions and cults, ritual sex change was a fundamental and sacred path for the priestesses. The goddess Atargatis was known in Syria as Ishtar, and by the Romans as Dea Syria. Followers of Atargatis dressed in the clothes and assumed the role of the opposite sex, in much the same way as Greeks worshipped some of their gods, goddesses and deities. Examples of Greek crossdressing figures are Achilles, Heracles, Dionysus and Athena. An illustration of the transferable nature of these deities is Dionysus, whose religious cult began in Greece and was picked up by the Romans, who then regarded him as Bacchus. We know Bacchus as the god of the vine, wine-making, ritual madness and religious ecstasy. Bacchanalian rites were orgies of indulgence where dressing in clothes of the opposite sex played a significant part.

Within these ancient societies there were pockets of unease, an example being that Hebrew males became preoccupied with establishing patriarchal rule. What this meant is that they were concerned with now making distinctions between male and female. I must clarify here that this wasn't something that happened solely in Jewish culture – it's just well documented within Jewish law, so we have clear evidence regarding how the distribution of goods, land and chattels between the sexes began changing; with the rise of patriarchal law and power, this was the end of matriarchal/communalist society.

With societal evolution, we as a species became more effective at providing for ourselves. We grew our own crops and began storing what surplus we didn't use. This had typically been a male responsibility, and under the shift in patriarchal rule men decided it was their right to keep hold of what was left over. When male elders died, any surplus was passed on to their male heirs (by contrast, under matrilineal law any surplus was owned by the community). These are the first examples of accumulation of wealth.

These changes are likely to have been small at first, but they were slowly transforming society. As men became richer, a divide between the 'haves' and the 'have-nots' became increasingly apparent, essentially between the men who 'owned' and the women and non-hegemonic men who did not. The rise of patriarchy created a ruling, or owning, class, who in turn created slavery.

This small owning class wouldn't be able to control the 'have-nots', so they developed laws requiring enforcement, and courts, prisons and armies were created. As this new social order grew, society was continually divided by inequality between the male ruling class, women and those who didn't fit the hegemonic male acceptable norms, including those whose GI was considered questionable. People grew more and more hostile towards gender diverse people, no matter what their status within society was (even those supposedly in power weren't safe). Two examples are, firstly, the Egyptian queen/king Hatshepsut, as illustrated in the book *The Woman Who Would Be King* by Kara Cooney (2014). Hatshepsut was queen but because of the now low tolerance of powerful females she spent her reign crossdressed as king as a means of survival. After she died, she was forgotten as quickly as possible. And then we have the Assyrian king Ashurbanipal. He was fond of crossdressing and it was something his court just had to accept. However, in the shadows there were those who conspired for his downfall; a crossdressing king was not a king who could be accepted. He was challenged, and when he refused to stand down, his city was sealed shut and he and all his subjects were starved to death.

As patriarchy rose and class antagonisms deepened, the oppression of women and the outlawing of trans expression and same-sex love became fiercer and more relentlessly enforced. As a species, we began placing certain values and assumptions upon sex and GI (i.e. we have come to classify female and femininity as being a weakness and it is identified with things that are of less value in society). And in some parts of the world GV is seen as something of an abomination or something that's not to be taken seriously, maybe a bit of a joke. Is this at the heart of transphobia and trans hate crime? Your clients are likely to have experienced disgust and disbelief aimed at them, they may have been demeaned, misunderstood at best, they may be feared, humiliated, repulsed, attacked and destroyed at worst.

Looking back, the strongest repulsion and intolerance towards gender diversity seems to have existed firmly within Western cultures. As Feinberg (1996) states, there is this separation between how native cultures embraced gender diversity, whilst white Western cultures seemed focused on destroying anything outside the gender binary:

> Why did many native cultures honour sex/gender diversity, while European colonialists were hell bent on wiping it out? And how did the Europeans immediately recognise Two-Spiritedness? Were there similar expressions in European societies? (Feinberg 1996, p.29)

What Feinberg is asking is, how did the European colonialists understand and interpret what they discovered when they encountered gender multiplicity within other cultures? We have examples of GV from Christian and Islamic faiths, and it is widely accepted that this is also true for many cultures throughout the world, going as far back in history where we have the recorded evidence. What is important to understand is that the reasons why individuals from various cultures came to cross the gender border are as varied as there are cultures where people do it. It is also important to note, and I will explore this in much more depth in Part 2, that the reasons for gender crossing are distinct and have a well-defined cultural history which is understood by all within the culture. As we shall see in the ways the colonialists treated any forms of GV when they encountered it, it would appear that our first-world Western societies lost whatever may have existed in terms of GV many hundreds of years ago and the effects of this are now being felt by the GV clients we may be working with.

Feinberg mentions colonialists treating with disgust the Two-Spirited (or Berdache, a derogatory term) people of the Native American nations they encountered. The colonialists' apparent low tolerance of anyone who presented outside of the male and female binary in their homelands would be extended with the same ruthlessness as they plundered the New World. So, what fuelled this level of hatred as people were initially acknowledged as sodomites and homosexuals? Again, it would appear there's embarrassment and misunderstanding, which we see expressed within our language; I believe that the majority of Western populations are confused about what sex, sexuality, gender and GI actually are. To illustrate this point, we can look towards ancestral cultures from around the world which have normalised what we regard as GV. These cultures have firmly embedded GV within their communities, beliefs and histories. GV is normalised and has a recognised place where its presence has meaning and significance, as we can see from this example by Professor of Human Sexuality Studies and Anthropology, Gilbert H. Herdt:

> Among the New Guinea Sambia, several criteria constitute the categorical *kwolu-aatmwal* ('female thing changing into male'). These traits include, for instance, anatomical ambiguity at birth; assignment of the infant to neither the male or the female categories but rather the *kwolu-aatmwal*; the existence of a lexeme and noun of the same name; a cluster of social attitudes about personal development and change; the existence of moral and social practices that constitute a different means of handling social life after puberty; and the autochthonous myth of parthenogenesis in the ancestors, whose first anatomical condition was hermaphroditic.
>
> The criteria define a symbolic niche and a social pathway of development into later adult life distinctly different from the cultural life plan set out by a model based on male/ female duality. Note again how the *kwolu-aatmwal* exist in a culture of extra-ordinary gender differentiation, with sexual dimorphism marked in humans and nature, according to the Sambia worldview.
>
> That such a categorical alternative exists at all is a true accomplishment, a partial victory of nature over culture – not as complete as the American transsexual who uses the wonders of medical technology to do so, but still rather impressive – such that we might be inclined to see it as a triumph of the third sex. And yet, in the Sambia scheme of

things, no classificatory distinction is tenable that separates sexual nature from sexual culture when it comes to these persons. (Herdt 1993, p.68)

The above excerpt is just one example of the many cultures that exist around the world where gender diversity was and still is an integrated part of society. Yet the situation was very different within Western societies where social forces established during the fall (e.g. religion and patriarchy) pushed it underground. GV became hidden, and with it a chance for an open natural history was gone and false beliefs filled the gaps, concealing a true understanding. Any sexual behaviour unlike the assumed norm was regarded as paraphilia, sexual deviancy, and something to be removed and treated. And so, we arrive at Krafft-Ebing's seminal work *Psychopathia Sexualis*.

Born in 1840, Richard Freiherr von Krafft-Ebing was an Austro-German psychiatrist. Amongst other subjects he was keenly interested in forensic psychiatry. He is noted as the author of the foundational work *Psychopathia Sexualis* (*Sexual Psychopathy*; 1997). It is a forensic reference book for psychiatrists, physicians and judges, and is written in an academic style to discourage lay readers. The author deliberately chose a scientific term for the title of the book and wrote parts of it in Latin to discourage the use of the book for purposes of titillation. It was one of the first books about sexual practices that studied homosexuality/bisexuality. It proposed consideration of the mental state of sex criminals in legal judgements of their crimes. And in its time, it became the leading medico-legal textual authority on sexual pathology. However, for the purposes of our interest, although it acknowledged acts of crossdressing (my language, not Krafft-Ebing's), these were only ever regarded as aspects of another diagnosis, often homosexuality. There is no acknowledgement of GI or crossgender identification. Although Krafft-Ebing's book makes for quite dated reading today, it would have been ahead of its time back then.

It wasn't until the early 20th century that the English physician, writer and social reformer Henry Havelock Ellis acknowledged and proposed that it is possible for a person to feel like the opposite sex, to adopt that behaviour, and even dress as the opposite sex. He developed the name 'Eonist' (after the 18th-century crossdresser Chevalier d'Eon) to refer to these individuals, and referred to their behaviour as 'Eonism'. He says:

> On the psychic side, as I view it, the Eonist is embodying, in an extreme degree, the aesthetic attitude of imitation of, and identification with, the admired object. It is normal for a man to identify himself with the woman he loves. The Eonist carries that identification too far, stimulated by a sensitive and feminine element in himself which is associated with a rather defective virile sexuality on what may be a neurotic basis. (Ellis 1948, p.210)

This acknowledgement is important because of the culture in England at the time, where there was a strong focus on family values and clear understanding of male and female roles. Homosexuality was regarded as sexual deviancy/ psychopathology, and those who pursued it were known as 'inverts'. If caught, the individual could expect to be punished by death. With this threat hanging over them, gay men had to be creative if they wanted to stay alive. Molly houses as they were known (taken from the verb 'molly', meaning to have homosexual intercourse) were one such solution where gay men could meet in some safety. We know from accounts of the time that some of the activities would involve crossdressing; individuals would adopt a female persona, have a female name and use feminine mannerisms and speech. It was normal for the men to call one another 'my dear', to hug, kiss and tickle each other as if they were unrestrained males and females, and to assume effeminate voices and airs. Crossdressing has long held a place within Western gay culture, as it still does today with drag kings and queens. The Mollies provide a confused representation of crossdressing which is a long way from those experiencing expressions of discomfort with their GI. So, when Ellis made the distinction that homosexual crossdressing was not the same as GI crossdressing, it was a significant moment.

Meanwhile, across the Channel in Germany, Magnus Hirschfeld, a German physician, sexologist and advocate for sexual minorities, was working to improve the lives of the gay population in Germany. In 1897, he co-founded the Scientific Humanitarian Committee, a group that aimed to undertake research to defend the rights of homosexuals and to repeal Paragraph 175, the section of the German penal code that since 1871 had criminalised homosexuality. Later, in 1910, Hirschfeld established the term 'transvestite' to describe people whom we now regard as transgender.

During 1931, whilst on a speaking tour of the USA, the Hearst newspaper chain dubbed Hirschfeld 'the Einstein of Sex'. He identified as a campaigner and a scientist, investigating and cataloguing many varieties of sexuality, not just homosexuality. He developed a system which categorised 64 possible types of sexualities, ranging from masculine heterosexual male to feminine homosexual male. It was during this work that he first encountered individuals who expressed a discomfort with their GI. What isn't clear is whether he was referring to transvestites, aka crossdressers or transsexuals. He later went on to write his seminal book on the subject, *Transvestites: The Erotic Drive to Cross-Dress* (Hirschfeld 1991).

In the spring of 1930, Dutch artist Einar Wegener arrived in Berlin to consult with Hirschfeld. Wegener had spent the previous 20 years living as a woman and was known as Lili Elbe. She approached Hirschfeld because of his work around sex and gender and wanted him to supervise her through a series of pioneering gender reassignment medical procedures. Unfortunately, Elbe died of heart failure following one of the surgeries in 1931. Her story was dramatised in the 2015 film The Danish *Girl*, starring Eddie Redmayne as Lili.

The rise of the Nazi party in Germany threatened Hirschfeld's work and his life. He was considered to be 'un-German', and after the Nazis took power, they attacked Hirschfeld's Institute for Sexual Science on 6 May 1933, burning many of its books as well as its archives. Little remains of his work to this day. Hirschfeld was out of the country at the time on a book tour of China. He was never to return to Germany and lived the rest of his life in exile in France, where he died. His ideas and research breakthroughs were taken to the USA by one his students, Harry Benjamin, who as we will see in the next chapter developed his work and ideas into something which we can recognise today as the bedrock of GI and its medicalised treatments.

EXERCISE 1: HOW WAS YOUR GENDER IDENTITY SHAPED?

Okay, let's take a break from the historical stuff and turn our attention to you. As I mentioned earlier, one of the purposes of this book is to encourage you to think about yourself and what you may have commonly accepted regarding who you are and how you came to be. Even if you find you know who you are GI-wise, at least you might understand better how you came to be the person you know yourself to be. So, make yourself comfortable, sitting with your feet firmly on the floor. When you're ready, let's begin.

Take a moment to think back over your childhood and see if you remember specific moments when you learned how to behave according to your gender role. For example:

- Maybe you were told to change your behaviour because 'Boys/girls don't behave that way!'

- Maybe you saw this happen to a friend or siblings.

Now think about a more recent time: Can you remember any moments in the past few years when you were reminded of how to behave according to your 'appropriate' gender role and/or sexual orientation? (*Hint:* This might be more subtle.)

Do you know of any personal experiences which illustrated how social forces tried to shape your sense of gender or sexual identity? If not, maybe you have observed this happening to somebody you know?

Make a note of your findings because we will be coming back to them in Chapter 9.

In Treatment I: Excerpts from my Phenomenological Therapy Journal

Setting the scene, the year is 1994. This is my first-ever venture into psychotherapy and I am attending sessions within the NHS. I have experienced a 'nervous breakdown' (as they are referred to at the time). I have been diagnosed as having depression and anxiety with Obsessive Compulsive Disorder (OCD). We are within the first few months of what is the luxury of open-ended psychotherapy (yes, the golden days). My therapist is a lady called Gina, whom I am very fond of — so much so that I have developed a bit of a crush on her but I haven't told her about this attachment. I later discover that this can be quite normal within therapy, within terms of the client building trust and allowing the therapist in close enough for them to be able to do their job. However, at the time the attachment/ attraction feels all too real and true.

Gina and I have been discussing the nature of what has led to my descent into madness (as I see it), and during these conversations it's become increasingly hard for me to deny to myself that crossdressing is something I do and to realise it is a significant part of me.

But first, I think I should fill you in on a few background details: my OCD was focused on thoughts that I was a corrupted and perverted individual merely by having the thoughts that I had. This was evidence that the thoughts were true. Add to this the guilt of knowing that I crossdressed and here was as much proof if it was needed that I was as corrupted as I felt myself to be. Please remember, dear reader, that at the time — yes, this is the age before the internet — information about such things as crossdressing (or transvestism) was incredibly hard to find and its trustworthiness was also of dubious repute. Often referred to as a 'paraphilia', it was often made clear it was something to keep to yourself and to be incredibly ashamed of.

We pick up the work as Mark (this is the name I used prior to transition, and some GV people refer to their now unused name as their deadname) attempts to address the incredibly difficult acknowledgement that he crossdresses and that this must be proof that he is as sick as his thoughts tell him he is.

GINA: What's wrong, Mark? You've been very quiet today.

Mark sits there, head lowered, and eyes fixed firmly on the floor. He says nothing. He feels a huge black mass of a pressure bearing down within him. This pressure is telling him to be honest and tell Gina something which could destroy everything...even himself.

Gina waits for a couple of minutes to pass before she tries again.

GINA: Do you not want to be here? [She pauses] If you're struggling today, we can always finish early if you like, and try again on Friday when we are due to meet.

This suddenly snaps Mark back into the room. He is shocked by the suggestion of having the session ending ahead of time, and the distress of having to leave Gina isn't something he wants. He feels he must save himself and say something, but he knows that what he is feeling is the pressure to say very uncomfortable things.

MARK: I'm err...bothered that what I might say will make you hate me.

GINA: That I may hate you? Why do you think I might hate you? Are you experiencing one of the compulsive thoughts?

MARK: No, nothing like that. It's more because it will mean that I am as sick as the thoughts are telling me I am.

GINA: But we have talked about the thoughts mark, and they are part of the OCD that the doctor has diagnosed. We know they are merely thoughts, however uncomfortable they may feel, yes?

MARK: You don't know everything about me, and I know that if I tell you this thing then you will have a different opinion of me. These thoughts are real, and you will hate me and refuse to see me. I know they are real because I do them!

GINA: Okay, I hear what you're saying, and I appreciate that it's causing you distress, I really do. But I would like to say to you that I've been working with clients for a long time and I honestly cannot think of a time when a client has told me something that's so very personal and important to them that it has shocked me. You might be surprised that telling me what is on your mind doesn't change the way things are here.

mark becomes angry because he feels cornered between the thoughts telling him to disclose and ruin everything and Gina's calm, possibly accepting position that he is hearing. The pressure has been building within him for days, going over and over what this moment might be like. Now it's here and it feels nothing like what he has imagined. He feels fearful and confused and trapped. Without warning, the huge blackness ruptures and his private guilt and shame become born into the world as with abject terror he finds himself saying the words.

MARK: I'm a transvestite... There, I've said it and you now know how disgusting I am, and I had better go now before you go tell the psychiatrist and he'll end the work. [Mark rises from his chair.]

GINA: Thank you for trusting me with that... This feels like a big step for us in building trust. How do you feel now, and would you like to talk a little bit about what it is like for you to crossdress? Perhaps you would like to sit down so we can talk a little?

MARK: What? How do I feel? But aren't you ending the session and telling the doctor?

HE FEELS A COLD SWEAT PASS THROUGH HIM AND HE'S SHAKING.

GINA: No, I don't see any reason to do that because of what you have shared with me.

MARK: But the book I read in the library said that people who do this are mentally ill and must be treated to stop them doing it. It said we are sexual perverts.

GINA: Well, I don't agree with what the book says, and I think it could help you if we explore what it must be like for you to experience the crossdressing.

Mark was to discover through his therapy with Gina that his crossdressing wasn't as abhorrent to the world at large as he had thought it was. This was his first time he had experienced acceptance of something he had carried a lot of guilt about.

Even now in the internet age and with far more resources available (if they are carefully selected) your client's first experience of acceptance of this disclosure will be fundamental to the trust building within the therapeutic encounter. And even if you have worked with several GV clients, remember you may be the first person this client has come out to. Also remember that their experience will be unique to them.

CHAPTER 3

THE 'JORGENSEN EFFECT'

There is little doubt that 2014–15 was a significant time for trans people in the UK and around the world. Transgender had its profile placed in the full focus of media curiosity by several events occurring around the globe. In the USA, ex-Olympian and gold medal-winning decathlete Bruce Jenner (also a member of the Kardashian family of the prime-time reality TV show) publicly and speedily transitioned to Caitlyn Jenner and onto the cover of *Vanity Fair*. She would later cause controversy by her out-of-touch comments about what it is to be trans. Many who criticised her believe her background and privileged social position mean she does not speak for the majority of trans people's experiences. In their eyes, the speed with which she undertook her transition does not reflect the fact that for most people undertaking transition it can take many years to be able to afford the process.

Meanwhile, across the pond in the UK, boxing promoter Frank Maloney also appeared to transition expediently into Kelly Maloney. She then stepped ahead of the media outing her and headed straight into the *Celebrity Big Brother* house. Kelly said on reflection that appearing in the house so soon following her transition led to viewers not seeing the best of her as she admitted she wasn't in a great place emotionally. She was welcomed by some in the house and clashed with others.

The hit TV series *Transparent* by Amazon Studios, starring Jeffrey Tambor as Maura Pfefferman, a retired college professor of political science who finally opens up to her family about always having identified as a woman, won several awards. Meanwhile the BBC aired *Boy Meets Girl*, its first sitcom about a regular trans woman entering into a relationship with a cissexual guy. The lead trans character was played by a real-life trans woman, Rebecca Root. This is something quite unusual as up until then the portrayal of trans people in the media has usually been played by cissexual female actresses. The show gained favourable reviews, and the UK trans population for a while felt proud to be taken seriously. The year 2015 ended on a relatively high note with the release of the film *The Danish Girl*, starring Eddie Redmayne as Lili Elbe (her real name was Lili Ilse Elvenes). Redmayne did a grand job in his presentation of Elbe. However, it does feel like a little backwards step to use a cisgender man to play a trans woman. The film was also criticised for being written similarly to forced feminisation erotica, obscuring the actual story of a historical trans person, and for being based on a fictional book that does not tell the true story of Lili and her wife Gerda Wegener.

There were also a selection of documentaries on various aspects of crossing the gender border. A couple of the most sensitively handled were those by Louis Theroux. He spent some time in the USA with a variety of trans children and their families. He sensitively explored for the viewer the variety of ways the children experienced their GI and how the families understood and came to terms and reacted to their young gender migrants.

On a more sobering side in the USA, there were 26 murders of trans women during 2015. The majority of these women were black African Americans. The various aspects of trans and GV – good, bad and otherwise – were becoming household topics.

You could have been mistaken for thinking that this was the dawn of a new era in our understanding of trans and GV with its rise in the public spotlight, but that wasn't the case. This had already occurred 63 years previously with a lady who went by the name of Christine Jorgensen. She was born George William Jorgensen Jr on 30 May 1926. She was the second child of a carpenter and contractor, George William Jorgensen Sr, and his wife Florence Davis Hansen. Christine grew up in a neighbourhood of the Bronx, New York City. She would go on to describe herself as having been a 'frail, blond, introverted little boy who ran from fistfights and rough-and-tumble games' (Docter 2008).

In 1945, she was drafted into the US Army. Following her discharge, it was noted that she became concerned by her lack of male physical development, and it was also around this time that she learned of gender reassignment surgery (GRS). This, it would appear, confirmed for her the road forward and she began researching the process of reassignment and started taking oestrogen with the assistance of a doctor who was a friend of a friend. She made plans to travel to Sweden where she planned to undergo the reassignment process. However, en route she stopped over in Denmark where she met Dr Christian Hamburger, a Danish endocrinologist. She went on to undertake hormone replacement therapy (HRT) under Hamburger's clinical direction, and sought permission from the Danish government to have surgery. This was granted, and she underwent both an orchiectomy (removal of the testes) and a penectomy (removal of the penis). Jorgensen returned to the USA and eventually obtained a vaginoplasty when the procedure became available there. The vaginoplasty was performed under the direction of Dr Angelo, with Harry Benjamin as a medical adviser. Benjamin would go on to play a significant role in assisting many others to access GRS because of his work with Jorgensen. Although Jorgensen wasn't the first to have GRS, she was the first to have GRS in conjunction with taking cross-sex hormones.

The New York *Daily News* ran a front-page story on 1 December 1952. Jorgensen was an instant celebrity. The first authorised account of her story was written by Jorgensen herself in a February 1953 issue of *The American Weekly*, titled 'The Story of My Life'. The publicity created a platform for her, and she used it to advocate for transgender people. She influenced other transsexuals to change their sex on birth certificates and to change their names. Christine Jorgensen's case is significant because, for the first time, it directly challenged society's definition of what one's physical sex is, but what Jorgensen had just undertaken had questioned that stability.

A full four years before Jorgensen met Harry Benjamin, Alfred Kinsey, a fellow sexologist, asked Benjamin to investigate a child who had stated they 'wanted to become a girl' despite being born male. The mother wanted help that would assist rather than impede the child. Kinsey had encountered the child during his interviews for *Sexual Behavior in the Human Male* (Kinsey, Pomeroy and Martin 1975). Kinsey and Benjamin had previously seen nothing of the like. This child rapidly led Benjamin to understand that there was a different condition to that of transvestism, under which adults who had such needs had been classified up until that time. The psychiatrists whom Benjamin engaged in the case were unable to agree on a path of treatment, so Benjamin eventually decided to treat the child with oestrogen, which had a 'calming effect'. He then helped arrange for the mother and child to go to Germany, where surgery to assist the child could be performed. However, from then on they ceased contact, much to Benjamin's regret. Following this, Benjamin refined his understanding of the subject and his treatment plan. His 1966 book, *The Transsexual Phenomenon*, was immensely important as the first large work describing and explaining the affirmative treatment path he pioneered (Benjamin 1999). Benjamin became so well known for his work in this area that he lent his name to the Harry Benjamin International Gender Dysphoria Association, which is now known as the World Professional Association for Transgender Health (WPATH).

There is one more individual whom I think it is worth becoming acquainted with because of their work within the area of GI: Robert Stoller was an American Professor of Psychiatry at UCLA Medical School and a researcher at the UCLA Gender Identity Clinic. He had psychoanalytic training at the Los Angeles Psychoanalytic Society and Institute from 1953 to 1961. Stoller is known for his theories regarding the development of GI and the dynamics of sexual excitement. In his book *Sex and Gender*, Stoller articulates a challenge to Freud's belief in biological bisexuality (Stoller 1984). Drawing on his extensive research with transsexuals and advances in the science of sex, he advanced his belief in a 'primary femininity', the initial orientation within individuals of both biological tissue and psychological identification towards a feminine development. This early phase contributes to a feminine core GI in both boys and girls unless a masculine force is present to interrupt the symbiotic relationship with the mother. Stoller identified three components in the formation of core GI, an innate and immutable sense of maleness or femaleness usually consolidated by the second year of life:

- biological and hormonal influences

- sex assignment at birth

- environmental and psychological influences with effects like imprinting.

Stoller asserted that threats to core GI are like threats to sense of self and result in the defences known as perversions. He believes perversion to be an unconscious aggression in the form of revenge against a person who, in the early years, made some sort of perceived threat to the child's core GI. We will be coming back to Stoller in Part 2 of the book when we come to consider our understanding of GI as therapists.

There is someone who often gets overlooked in the development of gender diversity's evolution in the 21st century. Her name is Virginia Prince, although she was born Arnold Lowman on 23 November 1912, in Los Angeles, California. At around the age of 12, Prince began crossdressing, at first using her mother's clothes. This is the most common behaviour in the life of a crossdresser. Prince regarded her transvestism as something very private, but the internal pressure it caused her became too much to contain, and like many of those who have crossdressed in private the draw of it became greater and greater until, at the age of 30, Prince consulted a psychiatrist. Dr Bowman's initial reaction to Prince's outpouring of her story was: 'Okay. So, what else is new?' The doctor said there were thousands more like her – he knew of at least 350 in New York alone! He went on to say she should 'learn to accept herself...and enjoy it'.

Prince then moved to Los Angeles and looked up the name of another crossdresser. This led her and several others to forming a loose-knit crossdressing club. It was then that she got her first idea for *Transvestia*, a magazine for crossdressers, and in 1960 the first edition was published. To give a flavour of the time, Prince was arrested for mailing pornographic materials (*Transvestia*) during the US postal service's crackdown on homosexuality. This came as part of the rampant paranoia during that time, as crossdressing was still a criminal offence. She was sentenced to three years' probation – meaning no crossdressing for that period. However, it was suggested that she could be allowed to provide educational talks about crossdressing, which she agreed to do. This was a turning point for her as the talks were well received and it resulted in her travelling around the USA delivering them. She is also credited with establishing support and advocacy groups for crossdressers. The most well known was Tri-Ess, which has become the largest and oldest crossdressing organisation in the world. Its structure formed the model for how other groups around the world were set up, including the UK's first group for crossdressers, 'The Beaumont Society'. Prince was also good friends with Dr Harry Benjamin, who gave Prince her first prescription for oestrogen.

Prince had some very strong opinions around gender and crossdressing. To some she was a gender crusader, and to others she was rude and controversial. In her view, if you're not transsexual, you're a transgenderist – a term she coined and uses to identify herself. In fact, she considers SRS a mistake for anyone, and doesn't really understand how someone would identify as transgenderist. She disagreed with another term finding usage in the LGBT community: 'queer'. In her view, it is as defined in the dictionary a derogatory term meaning 'unusual' or 'odd' (or as the Collins English Dictionary (2015) defines it, unnatural, dubious, irrational, mad, demented or even unbalanced). While Prince understood the need for a term to identify the breadth and uniqueness of those within the gender spectrum, she preferred a word with a more positive connotation. Her controversial reputation was never more evident than following her death in 2009, with a very mixed selection of views from those who knew her:

> This praise of Prince demonstrates with crystal clarity the gulf between those with classic transsexuality and transgender people.
>
> To us Prince was a monster...pure and simple. He hated transsexuals, denied our very existence, denied that SRS cures transsexuality. He spouted the most transsexualphobic words imaginable his entire life. He personally did infinitely more damage to transsexual women than Jessie Helms, Janice Raymond and Mary Daly could even dream of combined.
>
> I'm glad he's dead and wish his harm died with him.
>
> Admit I'm not a 'fan' of Virginia Prince. I don't like her homophobic attitudes, don't like her attitudes about transwomen and SRS and don't like her sexist attitudes towards women. I can't mourn her passing without acknowledging that. She was a gutsy, brave and forceful person who fought for crossdressing men when no one else would, and for that, I do give her respect. But I don't want her seen as representing 'our' community because, for myself as a transwoman, she didn't. Complex characters leave complex legacies. (Foster, 2009, comments)

Others were less harsh:

> While I share a lot of your negative feelings about Prince, I also recognise his/her activism for a very particular group of people at a time when it was problematic and even dangerous to do so. Virginia Prince created a structured community where there was none. Whether you or I are members of that community which benefitted from this (sounds as if neither of us is/are) isn't the point, we can still see the value to the participants involved while still criticising many of his/her other beliefs and problematic actions along the way. (Foster, 2009, comments)

Love her or hate her, it is clear she did much to raise the profile of crossdressers. As the following quote says, she was one of the first to raise the same questions we are still wrangling 60 years later: 'Why can't we give people the choice to be who it is, or what it is they want to be? And why does society get upset about males who wear dresses?' (Foster 2009).

What has happened since the 1950s is that GI has gone below the radar for the most part. Of course, there have been other transsexual individuals in the intervening years who from time to time appeared in the media, usually presented as the familiar 'man trapped in a woman's body' scenario. Other transsexual women reached a similar level of public interest as Jorgensen – the likes of Jan Morris, April Ashley and Caroline Cossey all had their five minutes of public attention before disappearing back into the normality of day-to-day life. But for the most part, society hasn't really taken much notice of transsexuals, and why should it? The patriarchal power play of the binary works and keeps the masses in check.

Over the years the public's perception of GI has occasionally been given a reminder that gender may never be that straightforward. The youth of the time have an identity to call their own and social sub-groups have emerged – Punks, New Romantics, Goths and Emos – and the 'gender bending' of

David Bowie, Prince, Pete Burns and Annie Lennox just for a while caused cissexuals and the binary regulars to raise their heads and smile, tut or ridicule what they saw.

Can you remember the first time you saw Ziggy Stardust, Boy George or Lady Gaga? Who were you with? What was the reaction (both yours and those you were with)? What did you think or feel? Were you impressed or embarrassed or something else?

We are familiar with gender bending by artists and entertainers such as Lady Gaga, Grayson Perry and Boy George. But it has long been a staple of stage and theatre dating as far back as Ancient Greece. The other main area for crossdressing occurs within the field of comedy, where the comedian mocks or is a figure of fun. I believe this is where the most damage has inadvertently been done towards those who experience gender dysphoria. We are not crossdressing; we are dressing in clothes that match our GI; we are not trans or transgender, we are transsexuals. But to the uneducated we are all the same; there is no difference between crossdressing, genderqueer, drag queen, pantomime dame and transsexual. To those unaware of life outside the binary this is where they will pick up examples of the bloke in a dress as a figure of fun and mockery, and this is where some of the roots of transphobia occur.

So, what is 'The Jorgensen Effect' (JE)? The JE is the phenomenon we have witnessed since 2014–15 in relation to the public surge of interest in alternative GIs. There is a strong parallel between the public interest in Christine Jorgensen's transition and that of Jenner and Maloney. Jorgensen's public transition triggered aftershocks that rippled throughout the USA and the rest of the world, striking chords with those who had been silently holding on tight to their gender secret. There was no trans community then. This was long before the Stonewall Riots, and if you wanted to remain safe you kept your head down. However, Harry Benjamin had openly assisted someone whom the trans community could identify with, and suddenly there was hope. The flood gates opened and Benjamin was swamped by request after request for assistance from the silent many. So, in 2014–15 when the Jenner and Maloney transitions hit the spotlight within a few months of one another, GI began garnering public curiosity and attention. But why?

This time the combination of timing – gender and cross-gender identity was one of the last strongholds of contemporary society to be challenged – and the availability of social media played a large part in spreading and sharing these stories, making them accessible to whoever wanted to read them. And platforms within social media such as Facebook meant anyone could have a place to share their opinions.

Whilst we have this apparent dawning of an age that appears to be challenging the old order of patriarchal power, I believe there is a darker side, which I believe we can see as transgender hysteria, with people appearing to be collectively and instantly claiming their GI rights.

We now live in a time where there is wide knowledge around gender diversity. The sources of information regarding this are very accessible and often feature as part of children's education. This has led to situations where young people, both online and in their peer group, have been exposed to a lot of media around trans matters from a younger and younger age. This, I believe, is part of the problem because well-meaning types are putting information out there which younger and younger children are accessing and the old problem of misinterpretation of the information becomes a very real concern. We will be coming to and taking apart this concern in Part 2 of this book. But what is the knock-on effect of this phenomenon?

Well, we now have a situation where the only GI clinic in the UK that works with children and young people (based at the Tavistock and Portman in London) has seen their referrals double in 2016, and it's claimed that in that year 800 children were prescribed hormone blockers. This situation gets worse when you consider that referrals for first appointments can take anywhere from 12 to 24 months. This will have an impact on the mental well-being of individuals seeking treatments.

Caitlyn Jenner and Kelly Maloney transitioned in such a public way that people who hadn't really considered what transitioning might be like got to see a blow-by-blow account. Neither Jenner nor Maloney have had a transition that most transsexuals can access or identify with. Both had the benefit of money to allow an expedited migration. When either of them speak out publicly on transgender matters, they are not regarded in a positive light by their trans and transsexual sisters and brothers because both have the privileges of money, position and power, which allowed them to bypass the frustration, humiliation and the mental anguish that your average transsexual person goes through trying to access a medical transition. In the years since Jenner and Maloney transitioned, both have made what appear to be thoughtless and controversial comments (Jenner made supportive commentaries to an anti-trans President Trump, and Maloney has made several homophobic statements), which has pushed them further away from the less privileged trans population either side of the Atlantic.

There had been some contemporary interest in transsexuality in the years leading up to Jenner and Maloney. In the USA, Laverne Cox, a transsexual woman, activist and actress, played a transsexual woman in the popular Netflix prison drama *Orange is the New Black*, while Janet Mock, another transsexual woman, writer and activist, was also active in challenging the public perception of gender diversity.

Jenner and Maloney could never have perceived the conditions, circumstances and timings that their respective transitions would have upon the world of GI. They unwittingly created a perfect storm, and when its effects made landfall, things would never be able to be the same again.

We will now look at the impact that the Jorgensen Effect has had on those who are gender diverse and what the future might be like for them.

In Treatment 2: Excerpts from my Phenomenological Therapy Journal

The year is 2005. Much has changed since the last time we observed Mark in therapy. He's had a couple of therapists since 1993 and we now join Mark working with a Jungian analyst named Elke. It would be fair to say that Mark isn't sure if he is happy with the therapy as he isn't sure it's the best approach for him currently. But he's sticking with it for now.

Since the last instalment Mark has been qualified as a counsellor for five years, and now he's working as a counselling manager within an inner-city 6th form in an Adult Education College in West London. He's accepted his GI, and he acknowledges he is a crossdresser. However, he gets a feeling from time to time that he really struggles to make sense of it and this is so emotionally painful with regard to his maleness.

Mark is describing to Elke what he has experienced in relation to his gender.

MARK: There are times when I experience feelings in relation to what I see.

ELKE: Can you say a bit more about what you mean? What do you see and then experience?

MARK: Well... It's not the same as looking at a woman and being sexually aroused because it's so very different, but to the uneducated eye that is how it might appear. But inside it is far from that. It's a sickening feeling, a hot wave of dread and loss that washes through me. And then comes the feeling of utter sadness and desperation.

ELKE: What do you recognise the desperation and sadness to be?

Mark goes silent... He knows the answer but again fears what its acknowledgement might mean. However, not everything is straightforward.

MARK: When I look at women, it triggers the reaction of dread and sadness. What also washes through are these thoughts...that I will never be like them, I am never going to be female... And it feels like a death occurs within me.

Elke is silent for what seems like an age, yet her piercing grey eyes are fixed firmly on him and she has a thin smile. Eventually she speaks.

ELKE: So, what do you take this to mean? That you wish to be a woman?

MARK: I think that if I could have choice over male or female, I would have chosen female, but as that isn't an option it's kinda pointless and the outlook feels very bleak.

ELKE: No, I understand that. But what about living as a female?

MARK: That seems impossible, and I don't even believe I look realistic as a woman!

ELKE: You're describing there being something other than the desire to wear female clothes, yes?

MARK: Yes, the feelings I have told you about seem to be getting worse and it doesn't seem to help when I do crossdress. At times, it feels as if this isn't the version of my life that I was supposed to have.

ELKE: But Mark, c'mon. You know there are many people out there who have lived gendered lives other than the one with which they were born.

MARK: What? Do you mean transsexuals?

ELKE: Yes.

MARK: Well, I'm not one of them.

ELKE: Okay. How is it you are so very sure of this?

MARK: I'm not a woman trapped in a man's body... I so hate that phrase. How does anyone know what that would feel like anyway?

Elke nods her understanding.

ELKE: Go on.

MARK: Look, I have read many stories about transsexuals in the papers when they crop up, and the person the article is based upon always says they felt they are 'a woman trapped in a man's body'. I don't think I even know what that would be like. So, if I cannot identify with that, then I guess I can't be transsexual?

ELKE: mmm... Okay, I hear what you are saying. However, I would like to clarify what you have told me today, so we are very clear in how things are for you. Okay?

Mark nods his understanding.

ELKE: So, today you have described to me a very challenging, potent, painful and intense phenomenon you've experienced throughout your life, when you cast you gaze upon a female. This isn't a sexual thought/feeling in the obvious sense a man might have when he looks upon and is sexually aroused by the female — you are not wanting to have sex with her. What you experience is more of a recognition/connection. Within that moment of the gaze you see something which resonates within yourself. Within that moment you see her femininity and it touches something comparable within yourself. Within that moment you are reminded of who you are within the world and how far that is from the sense you experience within that moment. As you gaze upon her femininity, your internal femininity cries out to be recognised within the world, to have a place to live and exist. But she is buried within the masculine. And then you experience the flood of dread and panic wash through you and everything feels pointless.

Elke goes silent and looks directly at Mark, with her eyes appearing oversized behind her thick-lensed glasses, the thin-lipped smile fixed in place as it usually is during the silences between them. Mark feels uncomfortable as what he's just heard feels very familiar. Not only because it was a recognisable set of feelings and thoughts… No; it was more that he had had them reflected back to him by someone who he wasn't sure had any idea of what he experienced. For a long time, it had been hard enough to come to terms with the crossdressing, but when he started experiencing this psychological and physical phenomenon he hadn't drawn a connection that they were part of the same thing. Why should he have? Coming from a background where he had all kinds of strange and at times uncomfortable thoughts, he hadn't drawn an obvious connection. In his experience, the crossdressing had usually been something he'd enjoyed once he got his guilt in check. But the occurrences which Elke had just described were far from pleasant. But somehow, which wasn't clear to him at that moment, the crossdressing and this phenomenon were connected. He couldn't understand the connection or make sense of what or how the two were connected, but what he did know, confirmed by a feeling he now had, was that they were indeed part of the same thing.

During that session, Elke described Mark's reoccurring phenomena, with the outcome that he for the first time drew together the two aspects of his experiences (i.e. the crossdressing and this physical and psychological phenomenon).

What was being explored and defined is what we now recognise as gender dysphoria. In 2005 this was not the definition which the **Diagnostic and Statistical Manual (DSM)** used. They only introduced the term in the 5th edition of the book (**DSM-5**) in 2013, when 'Gender Dysphoria' replaced 'Gender Identity Disorder'. Gender dysphoria is now the common clinical term used when making a medical diagnosis.

As a therapist, I believe it is fundamental to client work to explore what/how the client experiences their dysphoria. It's important to clarify that each client's dysphoria will be experienced uniquely to them. Although the DSM has specific clinical criteria that give details of the various symptomology that is considered essential when making a diagnosis of gender dysphoria, as illustrated in our second episode of Mark's therapy there is the possibility for the individual personal experiences to not sit quite so firmly on the rails of the DSM criteria. We will look at the individual's own experience in more depth in Part 2 of this book.

EXERCISE 2: PERSONAL MEANING – PART 1

Adapted from 'The Ten-Minute Gender Outlaw Exercise' by Kate Bornstein (1998)

Go through the questions and reflect upon what each means to you. It might be useful to make some notes as you go.

1. What does it mean to be male?

2. What does it mean to be a man?

3. Have you ever been treated like a man?

4. Did/do you enjoy it?

5. What did/do I enjoy about it?

6. If you're not male, what would you most like about being a male/man?

7. What does it mean to be female?

8. What does it mean to be a woman?

9. Have you ever been treated like a woman?

10. Did/do you enjoy it?

11. What did/do I enjoy about it?

12. If you're not female, what would you most like about being a female/woman?

Once you have your reflections, keep hold of them as you will need them in Chapter 9.

CHAPTER 4

THE AFTERSHOCK OF THE SECOND 'JORGENSEN EFFECT'

This has been an incredibly difficult chapter to write, because part of me wanted to write something which would capture the zeitgeist around gender as the landscape around GV currently has an overwhelming sense of continuous unfolding transformation, and hysteria. And while I want to give an honest sense of the situation, I am very reluctant to get caught up in the madness of what I have observed. On GV forums I've seen snobbery, back stabbing, bitching, in-fighting and a level of intolerance which I would have thought those so-called adults should have known better than to engage in. The behaviour often seems somewhat closer to that usually found in the playground. For a section of society which is no stranger to intolerance, one would have expected better between ourselves and our allies. One quite recent example was when my partner, who delivers my trainings with me and has been with me throughout my transition, and who I can say with certainty has played her role in educating others around GV and certainly would be an ally of GV people, made a comment on a Facebook post supporting a GV individual only to be verbally abused by someone quite unexpectedly purely because the piece of terminology she had used was now considered out of date. This felt unjustified and it demonstrated this intolerance. It was a harmless mistake (terminology is always changing) which could have been addressed in a calm manner and certainly didn't require such venom.

As I have highlighted already, there are preventable problems around the language being used around GV by the media. These create confusion and drive the hysteria which seeps into the popular culture that is fundamental in a lot of people's (both cis and GV) lives, in that many individuals connect and socialise online. It is my belief that for meaningful change to occur both the media and consumers of media must be responsible and considered in the language and terminology they use; only then may we see a reduction in hysteria. I fear that time might be some way off as the current proliferation of stories regarding GV – with it being portrayed as undermining and threatening the natural order of things in some part of society or other – shows no sign of abating. It goes without saying that most of these articles are predominantly written by cissexual journalists within the mainstream media who have little or no understanding of the reality of GI; their pursuit of selling units of media demonstrates little or no consideration for lack of accuracy and its impact upon GV individuals trying to go about their everyday business, access medical services and even live a peaceful life.

Week in and week out we get media stories which are more interested in political point-scoring or attempting to further wind up trans activists and TERFs against one another. This was the case during a recent Channel 4 series, *Genderquake*, which was a loosely based follow-up to a very-well-put-together and widely regarded series, *My Transsexual Summer*, which first aired in the autumn of 2011. The recent *Genderquake* series came in two parts: the first seemed very similar to *My Transsexual Summer*, with several GV individuals taking part, all of whom were exploring their GI, and concluding that gender is very confusing. This was followed by a studio debate, which seems to have been put together to create further controversy around GV. The guest list appeared to have put together curated to cause maximum shock and drama rather than encouraging a healthy and meaningful debate. The result was a missed opportunity and was far from balanced, with TERFs in the studio audience heckling one of the GV women panelists, saying, 'You're a man!' The guests included Germaine Greer, an old-school feminist whose outspoken opinions towards transsexual women haven't evolved since she wrote her book *The Whole Woman* (Greer 1999). A chapter in the book, 'Pantomime Dames', regards transsexual women as 'wannabe women' (pp.80–81) in a socially charged attack reflecting the widely held view that these are man-made women. The GV side included good-old Caitlyn Jenner. While she has a high media profile for a transsexual woman, there are many transsexuals who feel that Jenner's family wealth and status have enabled her experience of life beyond transition to be one that very few transsexuals can relate to or access. This has led to many saying that her opinions are not theirs and she doesn't speak for them.

Jenner has also struggled to be taken seriously due to her close association with Donald Trump's administration and his policies towards the treatment of GV people across the USA. In this regard, Trump has attempted to undo the progress of his predecessor, Barack Obama, in two especially notable areas: the rights for GV people to serve in the US military; and what has become known as the 'Bathroom Bill'. On 26 July 2017, Trump sent the following tweet: 'After consultation with my Generals and military experts, please be advised that the United States Government will not accept or allow Transgender individuals to serve in any capacity in the U.S. Military.' In a series of further tweets, he added: 'Our military must be focused on decisive and overwhelming victory and cannot be burdened with the tremendous medical costs and disruption that transgender in the military would entail.' There was understandable opposition to the initial ban, and in April 2018 the ban was altered; however, opposers said the two bans were essentially the same, and now a legal challenge will mean the ban is waiting to be contested in court.

The Bathroom Bill is the common name for a piece of legislation/statute which defines access to public facilities, specifically restrooms, by transgender individuals. This Bill influences access to sex-segregated public facilities for an individual, based on the determination of their sex as defined in some specific way such as their sex as assigned at birth (i.e. their sex as listed on their birth certificate). Technically, the Bill is exclusive of GV individuals, because if their GI differs from their birth certificate sex they will not be permitted access to toilets which pertain to the sex of their GI. Even more complex would be the needs of genderqueer or non-binary individuals.

Critics of the Bill argue that it does not make public restrooms any safer for cisgender people, and that it makes public restrooms less safe for both GV and cisgender people. Additionally, critics state that there have been no cases of a GV person attacking a cisgender person in a public restroom. By comparison, a much larger percentage of GV people have been verbally, physically and sexually harassed or attacked by cisgender people in public facilities. For these reasons the controversy over transgender bathroom access has been described as a moral panic.

Supporters of the Bill say such legislation is necessary to maintain privacy, protect the innate modesty held by many cisgender people, prevent voyeurism, assault, molestation and rape, and retain psychological comfort. So, what they are saying is that it is their belief that there is overwhelming evidence that GV people have a predisposition towards sexual deviancy and paraphilia – like those listed by Krafft-Ebing in his book *Psychopathia Sexualis* (1997) – and so much so that they cannot control their urges and will use the opportunity of entering toilets of the other sex to perpetrate these acts. This massive generalisation is fear-driven and uneducated, and I think I will treat it with the regard it deserves and move straight on. Before I do, I would like to point out that transsexual people have been using the toilets of their identified gender for decades. To be blunt, if a person has such paraphilic tendencies and is driven to act them out, they don't need a bill or law to permit them to go into a public toilet of the opposite sex – they will merely do this regardless if this is their predisposition. The reality is – and here I agree with the critics of the Bill – there is a greater risk to the safety of GV people using public toilets by some bigoted cis people.

While this issue has garnered much attention in the USA, here in the UK it is still a concern, but it appears to be a part of the wider topic of the reviewing process of the Gender Recognition Certificate (GRC). By way of a brief background, transsexual people have been able to apply for a GRC. If this is granted, the individual will be issued with a full certificate. This can be used as evidence of their new legal gender. The individual should almost never have to show this to anybody, and organisations should not ask to see it. Now this is where things can get confusing... Many transsexual people, by the very nature of their transition, require some medical intervention (e.g. hormones, surgery, or both). However, currently the Gender Recognition Panel (GRP), which decides whether a GRC application should be approved, states that for some GV people who wish to apply for a GRC the minimum requirement is that they change their name and live full-time in their identified gender. Confusing... I told you it would be. The British government initially suggested a less medicalised/legal intrusive process of Gender Self-Declaration, which many trans activists are in favour of. However, I feel less inclined to agree with this, as the letter I sent to the Prime Minister illustrates:

31/10/17

Dear Prime Minister,

Re: Consultation & Review of Gender Recognition Act

I have felt compelled to write to you following the announcement to begin the consultation regarding the 'New Action to Promote LGBT Equality'. [As] a woman with a transsexual background I am particularly dismayed by the proposals in relation to the review and possible dilution of requirements for the application of the Gender Recognition Certificate (GRC).

I appreciate that there will be those who look to the current requirements for the request and submission of a gender recognition application and feel it is a bureaucratic process that might appear intrusive, impersonal and clinical. And while I can appreciate that might be the case for some who desire to be publicly recognised with the full personality of expression, I think that watering down the process for the application for the GRC is not the way forward, and it will confuse the population of people it is designed to assist.

As a psychotherapist of 17 years' clinical experience I am very well versed that we in the West live our lives and have a strong sense of self-hood, and that we believe we should all be striving to attain and express our most authentic selves. I see clients daily (both trans identified and those who are not) who are in some way or another trying to gain a better understanding of themselves but are also trying to move towards [the] more honest, comfortable and complete version they can be. So, as you can see, in some respect this desire to be authentic and be recognised is something not exclusive to the transgender population. We can see throughout the decades various sub-cultures have existed as … each decade's young people have strived to own that decade and impress their own mark upon it with the likes of Mods, Rockers, Punks, Skinheads, Emos and Goths. Some of these have endured in some form over several decades. But what I think we are currently experiencing with some younger people under the current explosion within the LGBT movements is concerning because of individuals' confusion, and a collective lack of clarity. Why?

Well for starters I think that having the 'T' included as part of the LGB [acronym] is confusing as they are focused primarily around sexuality, whereas the 'T' is focused on Gender Identity. This confusion has I believe set GV people's chances of acceptance back some years. I stress I have no issue with the LGB population, but I think clarity here would certainly help. And I believe it [is] great to have organisations such as Stonewall now supporting trans people, but it also brings with it the possibility of confusion.

Secondly the language around GI is confusing at best. And nowhere is it more confusing [than] by the current use and misuse of the words 'Transgender' or 'Trans'. The words have essentially been used in such a way as to render them meaningless. Why? Well because transgender, and its shortened version trans, doesn't define anyone. They are umbrella terms that encompass gender diversity. Within that umbrella you then have your sub-groups, be they crossdressers, transsexuals, gender neutral, genderqueers, non-binary, etc., etc. NO one person is transgender or trans as they will ALL identify as one of the sub-groups. And the thing to consider here is that by their very nature sub-groups' needs will be very different. It is my unease that with the reviewing of the Gender Recognition Act (GRA) you [are] trying to resolve many differing matters with a one size fits all solution. The variety of the individuals and their respective needs will mean that the only solution is one that allows for an element of flexibility whilst providing robust boundaries. It is my belief that the needs of non-binary are very different to those of transsexuals. And whilst I agree 'being trans is not an illness', being transsexual and seeking some aspects of transition which [...] require medical interventions as part of the transition is in my mind a justifiable diagnosis. Without a diagnosis of gender dysphoria, the whole process of medical transitioning is little more than cosmetic modification, which for something as substantial as GV fails to provide adequate safeguarding. I would like to add that whilst I am comfortable with the provision of a diagnosis of gender dysphoria, I am less comfortable with any form of psychopathologising of gender variation, as this perpetuates a sense of GV being abnormal and nothing healthy will come from that.

As I am sure you are aware the GRA was set up to primarily enable transsexuals to bring into line the paperwork with their newly acquired GI. And yes, I appreciate that there are those transsexuals who are non-op and may have gone through with a GRC application. I should say that with all the transsexuals I have worked with over the years, none have complained at the process being intrusive and medicalised; on the contrary they appreciate that it is rigorous because unlike other forms of GV a transsexual is opening themselves up to a huge medical undertaking. Transsexuals by the most part are quite familiar to medical processes. If they do have a complaint it was about the amount of time it takes to get a report from the Gender Identity Service or the financial costs of the application. But I think the GRC process is set at about the right level as it is self-selecting, and I think that is a good thing. Most transsexuals feel comfortable in their gendered-selves that they don't all need a piece of paper to tell them who they are, and I question why someone who is transsexual [...] needs a piece of paper to validate themselves. Non-binary is not the same thing as experiencing gender dysphoria, and [...] it appears from my monitoring of trans forums that the majority of those who are wanting something done to the GRC application are not the main people who would have been applying for it in the first place. Their needs may well require a different solution.

If I may suggest ... it isn't the GRC process that needs updating but rather the addition of something else to address the needs of the genderqueer/non-binary individuals whom I believe are behind the pressure to get reforms made.

I have been contracted and in the process of writing a book on gender and gender diversity for therapists. And two things [that] have really struck me in the research of this book are: [firstly] the constant confusion around LGB and T. This confusion has been around [for] thousands of years and I hope the book might play a small role in changing that. And secondly is that the needs of the sub-groups under the transgender umbrella are varied. I do hope that this consultation will include talking to some of the many voices which exist under the umbrella, and I mean talk to them, not just use the survey, because I've completed it already and some of it wasn't relevant to me or my client's experiences.

Please Mrs May can we get this right before we do something which causes more problems than it solves.

Yours sincerely

M. A. Webb

Madison-Amy Webb
Accredited Dip Couns
MBACP, Voluntary Register
Counsellor/Psychotherapist
Supervisor/Trainer

Their standard reply thanked me for my letter and assured me that it would be forwarded to the Women's and Equalities Minister, a post which now has its third incumbent in two years. I don't see it as the place of this book to suggest a solution, but on this matter I shall conclude by sharing with you the title of the World Professional Association for Transgender Health's Standards of Care: *Standards of Care for the Health of Transsexual, Transgender, and Gender Nonconforming People* (WPATH 2012). I think that a possible resolution to this GRC reviewing process might be to remind ourselves that gender is varied and what WPATH acknowledges is that there are distinct sub-groups and that perhaps the one-size-fits-all approach which the UK government is wrestling with might not be the appropriate resolution, and possibly a multi-pathway model might be more appropriate.

The Problem with Diversity

Diversity of species on planet Earth exists… FACT! Diversity of races within the human species on planet Earth exists… FACT! And diversity of sexualities and gender identities within the human species on planet Earth exists… FACT! Evidence to support these statements can be found by simply going about our regular day-to-day lives. We share this planet with many differing species. We human beings come in all shapes, sizes, sexes, colours, sexualities, ages, states of well-being, cultures, intelligences, races, statuses, classes, faiths, etc. And our ancestors have lived with this knowledge since the conception of time itself. We are regularly reminded of these differences nowadays with the appearance of 'History Months'. I think these are valid efforts to educate people, yet I think they miss the point. For me, the issue is that by constantly pointing out diversity they reinforce the problem. Diversity is a 'red herring'. We know there are differences amongst our species, but repeatedly focusing on them reinforces the potential areas where conflict can exist. Saying there is difference doesn't stop fear of difference.

So here we are with this conundrum of our species: that anything other than the gender binary is questionable, isn't seen as acceptable, in some way lacks validity, and is fake and justifies being dismissed as either the product of a creative mind or mental illness. It feels like quite a disconcerting position when the majority of the species believes we are so advanced and far removed from the natural laws which actually govern *all* aspects of life; we stumble around in the dark, besieged by our fundamental belief in nature (i.e. that everyone is on the branch of the human species by our existence of birth, and therefore we automatically take a position on the gender continuum, whether we choose to accept it or not). Race, sexuality and gender are all aspects of being human which are subject to variation, so it can be said that they are all 'natural' by the very fact that they exist! We as a species have always railed against 'that which is seen to be not normal' – it's what we do. But the human species consists of many and we are varied.

In Chapter 2 we looked at the messages that have been fed to the masses over the centuries which support the construct of patriarchal privileges (i.e. women are acceptable, yet they don't have the privileges of men or the belief in a lot of fields that they are as good as men; therefore, if women want to find levels of equality, they appear to need to prove themselves).

Question: What is so important about these classifications that we become quite enraged when we're accused of not being a real man or woman? Let's explore this now.

When I first began preparing for this book, I originally used the word 'normal' before changing it to 'natural'. 'Normal' implies right and wrong, but with nature there is no right and wrong; there just *is*!

Despite our beliefs that we are an advanced, liberated, progressive species, there are GV people dying because there are some cis people in society who refuse to accept that there are some who don't feel they fit into the forced gender binary that their body has given them. These transphobic cissexual people believe it is acceptable to prejudice, harass, ridicule, harm and even kill GV people because having them in the world causes them to feel unsettled. As we saw earlier, the stronger ties GV has within non-Western cultures, with traditions and histories forming a fundamental part within the culture, act as a medium for GV people to be valued and have a meaningful place and purpose within that society. We in the West, with a decline in religion, social/folk traditions and confused cultural identities, appear directionless. And it's in this milieu that those who don't fit the gender binary can feel they have no social belonging and are devoid of a history. The reality is we all have a duty to establish our own GI. Without the societal tradition of valuing GV individuals, we are adrift without an established meaning (we will be exploring personal meaning further in Part 2 of this book), where all we are left with is the blind acceptance of patriarchal dominance and the promotion of heteronormative values as a false truth.

So, let me expand on why I see there is a problem with diversity. The first thing to acknowledge is that it isn't so much diversity itself, but rather the way that it has come to be paraded as some form of motif that will eradicate disharmony between differences. It's like saying that if we have diversity drummed into us enough times we will eventually reach a point of full and total acceptance of the rich variety and difference with which the human species presents itself on planet Earth. The reality is that the flag-waving of diversity will not resolve a great deal if it's not backed up by tangible and rational change to how we understand and regard GV. Let's be honest with ourselves: The human species isn't so fond of difference (this seems to be our innate, hardwired psychology), and in these more educated times even the most liberal of individuals will have a personal threshold of intolerance. We only have to look at human behaviour following 'the fall' (see Chapter 2) to see how many wars, disputes and persecutions have taken place over the millennia where groups and sub-groups within any given society have been scapegoated, removed and exterminated because of difference. I now want to illustrate, by way of a personal story, a view about human experience that is simple, obvious and overlooked.

In a dark part of my life, I was struggling with my identity, mental well-being and an undiagnosed gender dysphoria, without any hope of transitioning and living a life which was authentic and congruent. Like many going through hard times, I thought I had found solace in the bottle. Years rolled by, and the small amount of hiatus I thought I'd gained through drinking steadily became outweighed by the problems which it brought with it. I was in therapy in 2008 and came to the fearful acknowledgement that enough was enough and I had to do something about the situation before it began causing me bigger problems. This is how I came to find myself one evening in Clerkenwell, London, sitting in 'the rooms' as they are referred to by Alcoholics Anonymous (AA).

I sat amongst a diverse and disparate collection of people. We all looked like war-torn refugees who had temporarily escaped our personal battles with life and drink at least for the duration of the meeting. Now I didn't always agree with some of AA's philosophy; for example, I didn't agree that my drink problem was an illness over which I had no control. However, the service they offer is a great leveller. I've sat in rooms with an amazing cross-section of society – there were people from all walks of life, all colours and creeds, the publicly known and the unknown. Yet despite us coming from differing lives, we all had one thing in common in that we had fallen for this substance and made it our saviour from the pain and disappointments of our lives. At that time, I had been drink-free for around six weeks and was regularly attending several groups a week. I had been cautious of attending, having heard stories of god-loving dry drunks romanticising their drinking days and giving thanks through clinches and group hugs. That was a real turn-off for me, and very far removed from what I thought would be helpful in my recovery. I am certain my training as a therapist with an interest in existentialism/phenomenological principles has shaped my beliefs about theological concepts and how I 'experience myself in the world'. Alongside all this, I was aware that I was carrying a certain amount of shame, which constantly nagged away at me, that despite having thrown myself into my initial therapy and training I had still let drink get in under the radar and become problematic.

So, I gave myself over to the process and began attending these sessions several times a week; and then I came to experience a particular meeting which was to have a big impact on me. AA meetings would almost certainly have a guest speaker – usually this would be a regular member or someone from another AA group who would be handed the floor for 30 minutes to tell their story and take questions. I recall sitting listening to the chairperson of the meeting providing us with an introduction to the guest speaker. This is when they introduced a very simple matter for our consideration.

They suggested that while we were listening to the speaker we should try to hear and see the 'similarities' between their story and our own. The guest speaker was introduced and took the floor. A slim gentleman in his late thirties stood before us and in his very quiet and calm voice introduced himself as Rupert (not his real name) and began telling his story. He told us that he originated from Sudan and had made the journey to the UK during the Sudanese civil war. During the 1990s things got so difficult for him in Sudan that he and a friend decided to leave the country and seek asylum in the UK. He had lost his family, some of whom he feared dead, while others had become separated during the troubles. He arrived in the UK and sought asylum, and for an undisclosed period of time he was in the position of being stuck and powerless. Unable to work or sort himself out until he was granted leave to remain, he was living a very fragile and strained existence. It was during this time that he turned to alcohol as a means of managing the distress he was experiencing.

The terms 'alcoholic' and 'alcoholism' render the activity to a presumptive behaviour, removing any individuality. The Phenomenological Method (we will be undertaking an in-depth exploration of phenomenology in Part 2 of the book) would say that no two alcoholics will be doing alcoholism in the same manner, yet at the same time there will be consistent parallels within the individuals' experiences.

The chairperson invited us to try and see this by putting aside our obvious differences and instead looking at what connected us as people within the experience of human suffering and substance misuse. The Phenomenological Method asks us to do something similar and to put aside our prejudices and assumptions, as in the 'Rule of Epoché' (see Chapter 7), so we can hear the individual speak of their personal/human actuality of any given experience. We could look at this and ask, on the surface, what would I have in common with Rupert? Maybe very little; at least on a cultural basis, our lives couldn't be any more different. However, if we cut through the external packaging of the presenting person and do a bit of psychological archaeology, we see his human suffering, and here, despite the differences, we will find similarities. In that room in Clerkenwell everyone present with their unique experiences nodded in agreement when Rupert spoke of his utter despair, the isolation, the daily crying because he thought the emotional pain would never stop, the realisation that alcohol was making things worse and yet still being unable to end the cycle of addiction. I want to draw your attention to the similarities. The similarities of being human, the similarities of the struggles of being in the world, the similarities that we all have regardless of race, language, social positioning, personal beliefs, the family you have come from or not come from, your sexuality, sex and GI. As I quoted in Chapter 1:

> [W]e excrete, sustain our life force via nourishment, become emotionally attached to others, have the capacity to love and be loved, have sex for pleasure, can reproduce, can hurt and be hurt emotionally and physically, put substances into our bodies to feel different, become susceptible to illnesses, bleed and break, and ultimately all die.

Despite obvious differences, we are all more alike than maybe we care to feel comfortable admitting to ourselves. In my mind, the way forward means putting diversity to one side and beginning to focus on what we all have in common. We will have to open our eyes and look hard, and try to capture our prejudices before they jump in and tell us we are nothing like one another. The reality as I have outlined it here is that similarities are based in fact.

So, what has been the aftermath of the second Jorgensen Effect? The Jorgensen Effect from the late 1950s to the early 1960s showed the wider public that there was GV, and it was not always related to homosexuality. Christine Jorgensen demonstrated to other GV individuals that you *could* come out of the shadows, and there were professionals like Benjamin and the psychologist/sexologist John Money (1986) who were helping the transsexual population around the world. There would be a long way to go before GV became more commonly regarded. However, by the time the second Jorgensen Effect was initiated by Jenner, Maloney and others with their very public transitioning, we were living in an age where the media had grown and evolved exponentially. Information could be shared faster than ever before and on multiple media platforms. With the hunger for stories about anything unusual, the media's focus on Jenner, Maloney and others was merely click bait to sell units of media. It didn't matter if the stories were inaccurate or insensitive, just as long as they sold. Much like Christine had done 50 years previously, these public stories of transition showed a new audience that gender didn't have to be limited to the binary, or indeed that you had to disregard sensations of not fitting your body and possible feelings of dysphoria. Now you could come forward and possibly claim who you really were.

The problem was that societies around the world weren't prepared for the scale of what was about to hit them. Suddenly this wasn't just about a couple of people in the public eye fulfilling some strange urge which the general population didn't yet understand but soon would. Within a couple of years, the aftermath of GV had hit home and soon it would be someone's son or daughter, or brother or sister, or husband or wife, who was coming forward to put themselves on the gender continuum. Now there was a surge of people, both young and old, wishing to access medical interventions from limited and chronically underfunded gender medical services, which now found themselves awash with demand and waiting lists close to two years for access to the services. The recent public fascination with GV that has caused a surge in demand by individuals who feel a sense of developing their 'true selves' has forced society to question the gender binary normality and to question what has been commonly accepted for millennia.

And so, we have come full circle to the beginning of this chapter. We are far from resolving the difficulties and we appear to be in a state of hysteria about the acceptance of multiple genders. My biggest concern is that we are seeing missed opportunities for meaningful and balanced discussions around GV's position in the framework of the world. Time and time again I see click-bait-led programmes which serve as nothing more than some sort of freak show. This is doing more and more harm, and leading people further away from an innate and spiritual sense of GV (like that of the New Guinea Sambia people, and other traditional cultures). The treatment of GV has become a continual circus sideshow within the media and law, and this position furthers an 'us and them' stance whilst at the same time advancing GV into a disabling hysteria and preventing a healthy and positive evolution. This situation demands that as counsellors and therapists we must be diligent and not allow ourselves to get caught up in this folly; to stand back and not take on any of the current media hysteria that surrounds GV.

In Part 2 of the book I will focus on how we currently view, understand and do GI, and how Western psychology has majorly contributed to misunderstandings through its continued pathologisation of GV. I will unpick the zeitgeist and examine how it is further clouding the current societal understanding of GV. I will also explain why I believe there are some people who are getting caught up in the bandwagon of the second Jorgensen Effect, and are performing what I believe to be a pseudo form of GV where they confuse their core-self with self-expression, and as such have fallen foul of this media folly. I will offer some hope in the form of clinical methods, which if followed will counter this wave of media recklessness and will enable us as practitioners to implicitly aid the client to examine the core essence of who they sense themselves to be. I will also invite you to further examine your sense of GI with further exercises which will greatly prepare you for your own GV client work.

PART 2

TOWARDS A GENDER-POSITIVE MODEL OF THERAPY

In the book *Gender Outlaws: The Next Generation*, by Kate Bornstein and S. Bear Bergman, American transactivist and writer Julia Serano says the following:

> If one more person tells me that "all gender's performance" I think I'm going to strangle them. Perhaps what is most annoying around about that sound-bite is the somewhat snooty "I-took-a-gender-studies-class-and-you-didn't" sort of way in which it is most often recited, at magnificent irony given the way that phrase dumbs down gender. It is a crass oversimplification, as ridiculous as saying all gender is genitals, gender is chromosomes or gender is socialisation. In reality, gender is all of these things and more. In fact, if there's one thing all of us should be able to agree on it's that gender is a confusing and complicated mess...
>
> Sure, I can perform gender: I can curtsy, or throw like a girl, or bat my eyelashes. But *performance* doesn't explain

why certain behaviours and ways of being come to me more naturally than others. It offers no insight into the countless relentless nights I spent as a pre-team wrestling with the inexplicable feeling that I should be female...

When we talk about my gender as though it were a performance, we let the audience—with all their expectations prejudices and presumptions—completely off the hook. (Bornstein and Bergman 2010, p.85)

For many GV people one of the most compelling aspects of their journey to authentic GI is the desire to access the clothing (not usually acceptable to them within their respective culture) which they are likely to feel comfortable with. If you were to ask them what it is regarding this item of clothing that they feel drawn to, you would obviously get a variety of answers, yet within the answers they are likely to speak of forbidden fabrics, textures, materials and specific gendered items and the sensory relationship they have upon the skin.

EXERCISE 3: AN EXPLORATION – THE DRESSING-UP BOX

This exercise may take you out of your comfort zone; if so, that's okay – trust in the process.

I would like you to take yourself on a visit to your local charity shop and browse their clothing, shoes and jewellery. Allow yourself to become curious about the items on display. Let any boundaries you may have fall away and try not to see the items as male or female but rather merely as clothing and accessories. Remember, these things in themselves are genderless – it's us who place gender on them. Clothing comes in differing styles, fabrics, colours, shapes, sizes and textures. Look at clothing you have never looked at before.

Take it off the hanger and explore it. Turn it over, and look inside. What does it feel like? If budget and courage permit, maybe you could allow yourself to buy the item (this will make the next stage easier to do). If you feel uncomfortable about purchasing the item, ask yourself why that is. If purchasing it isn't an option, I would recommend that you ask if you may take a photograph of the item. Once you have the item home, hang it up somewhere visible, or if you have a photograph print it out and place it where you can see it over the coming days.

Become familiar with the item – study it again. Ask yourself:

- What is it about it that you were drawn to?

- Why did you select it?

- What does it say about you?

Make some notes and put them aside for Chapter 9.

CHAPTER 5

UNDERSTANDING GENDER?

Who in the world am I? Ah that is the great puzzle!

(Lewis Carroll, 1865)

I want to begin this chapter with another quote from Julia Serano. In her essay 'Performance Piece' she says: 'So, don't you dare dismiss my gender as a construct, drag, or performance. My gender is a work of non-fiction' (Bornstein and Bergman 2010, p.87).

Serano is saying that her experience of her GI is a fact and is based on her ontological (the philosophical study of the nature of being, becoming, existence or reality) experience, and it's hers alone. GV people, like everyone else, are real people living lives as experienced ontologically. They are not a construct for a theoretical hypothesis (we must not confuse this with theoretical methods of enquiry, such as phenomenology); these methods assist our clients to explore the meaning of their GI, and we shall come to these shortly. There's nothing Serano and other GV people (including myself) dislike more than when some well-meaning cis clinician attempts to theorise how their GI came into being or tries to figure out why there are some people who apparently rail against gender binary or see GV as a mental illness or a defect from their psychosexual development.

Gender can be comprehended in many ways, but theorising GV with a GV client is offensive as it adds to an 'us and them' status where GV is seen as different to the cis norm, and this will impact on building therapeutic trust. The thing to be mindful of is that there is no GV or cissexualism; rather, with regard to gender/GI, we ALL inhabit a position on the gender continuum. The exercises contained within this book are intended to demonstrate the nuances of one's GI and to allow readers to begin to understand some of its tonalities within themselves. I think now would be a good time to return to, and have a comprehensive look at, what endocrinologist Harry Benjamin said when observing our bodies at a physiological level:

> Just as the anatomical sex is never entirely male or female (one must recall the existence of nipples in men and of a rudimentary penis, the clitoris, in women), so is the endocrine sex 'mixed' to an even greater extent. Testes as well as the male adrenals produce small amounts of oestrogen. Androgen, in distinct traces, can be found in the ovaries and in the larger amounts in the adrenals of females. Their metabolic products can be identified and measured in the blood as well as the urine.
>
> Therefore, it can well be said that we are all intersexes, anatomically as well as endocrinologically. But we are male and female in the anatomical or endocrine sense, according to the predominant structures or hormones.
>
> The diverse amounts of both sex hormones in both sexes can have their influence on appearance as well as behaviour, the appearance, however, largely determined by the genetic constitution, the behaviour also by environmental and educational factors. (Benjamin 1999, p.8)

If further evidence is required as to the intersex nature of the human species, let's look at the results from the latest neuroscience research conducted by Georg S. Kanz of the University Clinic for Psychiatry and Psychotherapy of the MedUni Vienna late in 2014:

> Our sense of belonging to the male or female gender is an inherent component of the human identity perception. As a rule, GI and physical sex coincide. If this is not the case, one refers to trans-identity or transsexuality. In a current study, brain researcher Georg S. Kanz was able to demonstrate that the very personal GI of every human being is reflected and verifiable in the cross-links between brain regions.
>
> While the biological gender is usually manifested in the physical appearance, the individual GI is not immediately discernible and primarily established in the psyche of a human being. As the brain is responsible for our thoughts, feelings and actions, several research institutions worldwide are searching for the neural representation of gender identity.
>
> In a study under the guidance of Rupert Lanzenberger of the University Clinic for Psychiatry and Psychotherapy of the MedUni Vienna published in the *Journal of Neuroscience* it was now possible to demonstrate neural correlates (analogies) of the identity perception in the network of the brain.
>
> Trans-gender persons as well as female and male control subjects were examined by way of diffusion-based magnetic resonance tomography (MRT). The examination revealed significant differences in the microstructure of the brain connections between male and female control subjects. Trans-gender persons took up a middle position between both genders.
>
> It was furthermore possible to detect a strong relationship between the microstructure connections among these networks and the testosterone level measured in the blood. Lanzenberger: 'These results suggest that the gender identity is reflected in the structure of brain networks which form under the modulating influence of sex hormones in the course of the development of the nervous system.' (ScienceDaily 2015)

The above research was the latest in a series of three similar studies dating back to 2010, with all of them delivering similar results to Kanz's study. We now have several scientific examples providing physical evidence that GI is more nuanced than ever before. This study reinforces what Benjamin had said some years previously (Benjamin 1999), but what is key to consider is that both these studies and Benjamin's previous research apply to every one of us. Every single human that has ever lived, is alive at this moment and those yet to come are all located on what I now refer to as a GI spectrum. The concept of viewing GI as a spectrum has been around in a formal visual sense for a few years. If we now consider the biological sex classification of the spectrum to include this universal intersexuality, we will have to acknowledge that from an endocrinological position our current understanding of the male and female binary may only really apply to a very small percentage of the human population. It is very likely that chromosomally and hormonally there might only be a tiny amount of people who we can really class as a binary male or binary female. How often in life have you met someone whom you recognised to be either male or female yet there was something about them that didn't sit fully with that recognition of their apparent sex? Maybe they were a man with something feminine encased in their masculinity, or perhaps there was something male running through their female presentation. The fact is, we will never know endocrinologically how many male men and female women there are. But what we must now consider is that, within the biological sex classification, what we consider to be intersex is probably the far largest part of the spectrum, and what we have considered the binary may now actually be a minority!

Okay... Let's take some time to reflect. Has the last paragraph sunk in? Be honest with yourself... If not, maybe go back and reread.

Do you now have a sense of us living in a society where technically many people are intersex? I guess your life will continue pretty much as it has always done; nothing major is likely to be different.

But what about if you consider yourself on an infinitesimal level...the small stuff that makes you who you are... Suddenly, what you thought you were made of or what made you aren't quite the same... I'm wondering what that is like for you to know.

I'm wondering how you are feeling about the fact that you and I are very likely hormonally intersex. You may be cissexual, or you may be like me and GV, and there is a very strong possibility that you aren't part of the small percentage of people where their sex and hormones correspond.

I'm wondering what this knowledge may mean to you as a therapist working with clients dealing with their GI. And do you feel any different in yourself in dealing with clients questioning these kinds of topics?

What I have outlined above could change a lot of what we thought we understood about ourselves. The incorrect knowledge that's been presented via many conduits, be they medical, religious or sociological over the many generations, has meant we have been existing in societies which have not had an accurate understanding of our very nature/make-up.

Now, that was the easier part of the classification to comprehend, but there is still GI and gender expression for us to consider, and that part is not as straightforward as addressing biology. Treading carefully going forward here is imperative, so we don't make the same mistakes made by many clinicians and theorists who have travelled this same pathway in previous decades. Although theories are reasonable for consideration, I think they can easily side-track us down a path that takes us away from the most important person in any clinical encounter – the client – and in the case of this book an individual questioning their GI. Two examples of where theories are applied in a too generic way are as follows.

Firstly, the rather common and outdated belief that transvestites (now known as crossdressers) develop the behaviour often as a response to a longing for a mother they lost when young or who was cold and unemotional. By dressing briefly in women's clothing, they 'become' the mother they wish they had. So, all men who display that behaviour have mother issues. I would say possibly some do but not all. The trouble with this belief is that it throws everyone under the same label and behaviour classification and doesn't allow for individuality and personal meaning.

Now let's look at the second example of when theories get it badly wrong. Let us consider the psychoanalytical concept of 'primary femininity' as a second case in point. The idea of a primary femininity was proposed by psychoanalysts in opposition to Freud's original theories of female psychosexual development, which were founded on notions of a primary masculinity. For Freud, the development of the little boy and the little girl were identical at first, as captured by his now infamous words 'the little girl is a little man' (Freud 1933, p.118). He asserted that until the age of three or four neither the girl nor the boy has any knowledge of sexual differences or of the existence of the vagina (Freud 1925). Both the girl and the boy go through a pre-oedipal 'phallic stage,' with phallic, masculine sexual aims focused on the mother. The little girl's sexual sensations are concentrated in the clitoris, which was conceptualized as analogous to the penis. Moreover, Freud (1905) stated that libido itself was 'masculine' (p.219). Thus, the girl's sexuality begins as masculine and her future development depends on a reaction to, or a renunciation of, the original primary masculinity. Penis envy, her reaction to her lack of an adequate organ, initiates both the triangulation of her object relations and the turn toward oedipal interests, and forms as well the motivational basis for the wish for a baby. In Freud's account, the course of feminine development toward heterosexuality and motherhood was extremely convoluted. These formulations did not include ways to think about how a positive sense of self as female, of agency over sexual pleasure, or of pride in the female body might develop, or develop easily. (For a thorough discussion of the question of agency over female desire, see Hoffman 1996.) (Kulish 1997, p.1357)

Okay, let's take stock of what was covered here. The most obvious point is that Freud's theories only consider a developmental outcome of a heterosexual male and female binary. Now as we saw in Part 1 of this book, there were the beginnings of acknowledging GV at around the time Freud was considering his psychosexual development, and we only need to look to the work of Havelock Ellis and Magnus Hirschfeld to know that there was knowledge of something other than man and woman. Also, if we are going to give any credence to Freud's concept of primary masculinity, we need to consider two things: firstly, at the time psychoanalysis was an extremely patriarchal activity and, as such, a male-dominated occupation; and secondly, psychoanalytical theories were heavily influenced by the society of the time, whereby there was primary valuing of men and anything masculine-orientated, and by default women and anything non-male were considered of secondary value and importance. It was still a crime to be homosexual, let alone to consider that a man might consciously wish to relinquish his patriarchal rights and privileges and be willing to defect to an apparently second-rate sex. There is a term currently doing the rounds – effemimania – which is the cultural obsession with anything focused on male femininity. It is underpinned by traditional sexism, and that femininity is inferior to masculinity. This, I believe, has resulted in two things: firstly, I think it is one of the roots of transphobia; and secondly, I think it is why we have far more media interest in trans women (men who transition to females) rather than trans men (those journeying in the opposite direction). It is my opinion, based on my research and exploration within these matters, that while trans men may still be an oddity to some within the cissexual population, they can be regarded as at least knowing where they would be better off and aspiring to patriarchy, and as such they are more tolerated by cis hetero men. In the eyes of staunch patriarchs, or hegemonic males, a man who identifies as a trans woman must be insane to wish to give up so much privilege and power to join a perceived weaker societal group.

TERFs and Trans Extremists

At the time of writing there have been altercations between trans activists and some feminists known as trans-exclusionary radical feminists (TERFs). TERFs don't dispute GV people's right to exist; their concern is regarding the acceptance and validity of GV women as real women, and the impact of the integration of feminine-orientated GV upon birth-sex females within society. Their concern is that these feminine-orientated GV people cannot be true women due to them having experienced male privilege and having a male brain (it would appear they have not been made aware of Kanz's brain studies). They believe that if GV females infiltrate feminine spaces this could be putting birth-sex females at risk. They also believe that men might misuse this situation to get close to women in toilets and changing rooms. Opinions have run high and led to physical violence because a small sub-group of trans extremists wish to impose their definition of reality and their political agenda onto society, which in this case is that GV women are to be regarded in the same way as natal women (i.e. to suspend knowledge that a GV woman has entered the world in a male form). So, are they implying that GV women are to be regarded as biological women? If this is the case, then surely the argument falls before it even gets going with the acknowledgement that they are fighting their cause from the trans extremist corner? You cannot pick and choose when you are and are not GV, if that is the position you are coming from.

An interesting point for personal consideration is: how do we as practitioners manage this kind of extremist view if we discover our GV client holds these kinds of beliefs? Maybe the following might assist in understanding the position you might take.

Personally, I don't have a problem with coming from the position of GV, or 'trans' as they choose to refer to it. I acknowledged long before I transitioned that no matter what I did to my physical self in terms of feminisation, there would only be so much I could do to change my appearance and that would have to be enough; it was never going to change my birth sex and my life history (I never hated my male self in an extreme way, rather I never felt comfortable in the role of a traditional Western male). My concern is that this minority group of trans extremists might damage the improvements that are being made by various groups, services and individuals for the greater good of GV people everywhere. And while I think it is important that we as clinical practitioners provide our GV clients with the opportunity to explore and define for themselves their experience of the body they inhabit and the discomfort it causes for them versus what they sense about themselves, I also try to introduce a healthy balance of realistic expectations about what can be achieved through a medical intervention. With the best will in the world, a 40-year-old male isn't necessarily going to be able to transition into an 18-year-old girl. The best they can expect is a 40-year-old woman. And as important as recognising this is, it will bring with it an unwelcome disappointment because they are likely to have an internal image of the girl who they sense themselves to be and is not going to be able to come into being. This is what concerns me the most in the actions of the trans activists. Whilst I agree on having space to argue for being treated fairly in society, in my opinion it is unreasonable to push beliefs that you can be whoever you believe yourself to be and that it is society's place to accept that unquestioningly.

The trans extremists appear to be endorsing and forcing (including the use of physical violence) a form of societal delusion, and claim that anyone who doesn't accept their beliefs is being transphobic. If we want to live in a society with free speech, then we need to accept that we will sometimes hear things we disagree with or don't like; we cannot have it both ways. I think wherever these sorts of behaviours appear, they are extreme and out of touch with the reality of the situation experienced by many GV people; it's not good and they certainly are not speaking out on my behalf. I think this collective has found something to bond over, but I sense it is missing the point of what it is they are really struggling with. I wonder if this activism is serving some other personal purpose. A trans activist forum I was invited to join following a Radio 4 interview I gave has proved to be quite insightful. Whilst the members seem to be focused on lots of current and (as they see it) challenging issues, they also seem to be quite sad and unhappy with their lives. I'm aware I know very little else about them, but they do appear to be heavily involved with passing the misery around between one another. I guess there must be some form of bonding there for them in uniting behind a cause. For me and the clients I've worked with, transitioning was about improving the quality of our lives. And whilst a stress-free life doesn't exist, I think it's important to pick one's battles.

Primary Femininity as Gender Identity

For some the process of arriving post-transition (whatever that means to the individual) can be a bit of an anti-climax. Why? Well, firstly, what happens next after you have arrived at something close to your actualised self? For most transsexuals it's about moving on and living life, and like for the rest of society that can be mundane and is full of the things we all must deal with, both good and bad. For me that's usually a good sign that the individual has arrived at the place they needed to get to in order to feel complete and contented, and that they are now living in an authentic manner. If you think that post-transition is all about excitement and a continual thrill, you could be disappointed. A GV woman posted on social media a year or two back that if you think transitioning is going to make you happy and that you will have a trouble-free life from now on, think again, as you will be disappointed. Yes, post-transition you hopefully won't have the gender dysphoria to deal with, but you will have the life struggles that the rest of society all have to deal with. There are many days when I forget about my GV status (mainly before I started writing this book!), and for me that is a sign of personal contentment. I go and do the food shop and I am a regular woman picking up the week's groceries. This has a beauty to it because this is part of what I wanted to achieve. I go and put fuel in my car, and as I go to the kiosk to pay, a guy holds the door open for me and, smiling and gesturing for me to go first, says, 'There you go, love.' Maybe I'm old fashioned at heart but, in the dark days of not sitting comfortably within my male identification, I never dreamed I could achieve a sense of tying my inner and outer selves together. This seems to me to be far removed with what the trans extremists are concerned with, as they still appear to be seeking a sense of validation externally from others, rather than fulfilling their own needs and being comfortable with that. That is nice if it happens, but we cannot depend on it if we are seeking this as a basis for our happiness. Person-Centred Therapy theory regards this as living one's life governed by an external locus of evaluation…but more of that later. Okay, let's explore further the development of primary femininity. Bear with me as this gets a touch convoluted in places, but I think it is important to take this psychoanalytical diversion for a moment. As Kulish (1997) explains:

> The term primary femininity was originally used by Stoller (1968) in his studies of the development of core gender identity and its disorders. First, he attempted to counter Freud's notions about the primacy of masculinity, which had rested in part on a nineteenth century view of embryology. In Freud's time it was thought that the sexual organs were originally male, and that the female organs differentiate from this

original form later in foetal development. Hence, masculine sexuality was seen as the primary state. Stoller (1976) pointed out that modern embryology tells us the opposite: with the secretion of testosterone, male sexual organs differentiate from an original female configuration. In that sense, it is femininity that is 'primary': at least if one is going to use that kind of teleological reasoning. Stoller then argued that femininity for both females and males was primary in another sense as well, in that the first object of identification for the infant is female, the mother. Stoller (1975) also applied this concept of primary femininity to the psychology and the psychopathology of males. Here the concept of primary femininity is a particular kind or state of object relatedness.

Like Greenson (1968), Stoller suggested that boys have the difficult task of dis-identifying from their mothers in establishing their gender identities and sense of masculinity. That is why, he thought, more men than women are transsexual, or manifest other gender identity disturbances. Stoller's work on core gender identity also reflected ideas of primary femininity. 'Core gender identity' refers to the most basic sense of being a male or a female, which is now known to be set early, at about eighteen months. Stoller (1968, 1972, 1976) argued from a large body of research that different sources contribute to gender identity: inborn biology, sexual assignment, parental attitudes, learning and conditioning, and the body ego. He hypothesized that core GI is largely a matter of learning, based on parental assignment and developing out of the conflict-free sphere of the ego. In this view, the first conviction a girl has of herself as a female is free of conflict. Stoller did attend to the role of conflict and defence, however. For example, he wrote (1972) that the repudiation of femininity in men and the girl's wish for a penis are to be conceptualized as defensive manoeuvres, not the biological bedrock that Freud imagined. (Kulish 1997, p.1358)

Okay, let's take a moment to consider what is being said here regarding becoming aware of one's own body. I think this is important due to the acknowledgement by some younger GV individuals that they knew about their GV from a very early age. This concerns and confuses me. In my own dealings with clients exploring their GI, all but one appeared to have experiences that led them to explore their GI early on in their lives. The GV narrative follows a similar developmental evolution, and even though each will have their own specific personal touches there are certain key stages, both of which I will cover later. I can say in all honesty that what I sensed about myself in my early childhood, in terms of what I now recognise as an adult experiencing my GI, didn't present itself in any way as a recognition that I was in the wrong body. To this I would add that many GV individuals (myself included) whom the medical services would categorise as 'secondary transsexuals' (i.e. they transitioned later in life, roughly late thirties onwards) acknowledge a sense of something not feeling right, or something that didn't sit comfortably within them as to how they experienced themselves. And for many it wasn't even a question of recognising that their GI was out of alignment; it was a nameless discomfort within them. Despite this, not one of them described the now clichéd 'woman trapped in a man's body' or even applied the words 'transsexual' and 'trans'. What they often describe is something more subtle: an attraction to the clothing of the opposite sex, the texture, the feel of it against the skin, how the fabric changes the way they feel in themselves once it is worn on the body. If they put on shoes, these will force the body's posture to change. Heels will straighten the whole of the legs and the body, pushing the chest out. This is a very unusual sensation the first few times, but even though it's tricky, it conveys something which feels right for the individual. I cannot speak for what the experience is like for someone who crossdresses for pleasure into male clothes, but I would imagine it is going to be somewhat similar in a relative way.

I can clearly recall that in my early experience (up until the age of ten years) of what would later become crossdressing there was never a moment of it being related to GI. It was always a sensory maelstrom I was caught within. It was never so clearly delineated as at the beginning. I remember a fascination with textures, fabrics, colours. The knowledge that the clothing I was exploring was typically associated with the opposite sex caused confusion and guilt, but I believe that was more about them not belonging to me. I never consciously felt confusion with my GI or that I felt I should have been a girl or woman. I must add that I never experienced disgust over my genitals. They were part of me and I recognised them as such. That's not to say that as I developed into a young man I shared the same pride of possession for my male member as my contemporaries. And yes, I would visualise what I might look like without the male form in place.

As we saw earlier in my therapy journal ('In Treatment 1'), the years passed, and the crossdressing continued and evolved into something which reflected a wish to acknowledge a femininity. If this hadn't been subjected to the overwhelming confusion which came with puberty, I think the development of my GI might have been less confusing for me. However, as puberty arrived in my life, it set off a tsunami of hormones which would be my body's final act of physical, physiological and mental maturation. The hormones surged forth and collided with the crossdressing in what became a perfect storm. Suddenly, what was once quite a harmless activity became absorbed by the upsurge of hormones and took on a different and frightening edge of arousal and sexual fervour. Crossdressing had never been like this before; now it was a demanding beast that I had no control over. I remember time and time again trying to keep the crossdressing unsexual, but the hormones always won. I couldn't, and didn't want to, stop crossdressing, but every time the hormones turned it into something I had no real understanding of, other than that I was racked with guilt afterwards and had a sense of being perverse.

It would be many years later, after my initial disclosure to my therapist, Gina, and many tentative attempts at trying to have a guilt-free conversation about it with several other therapists, that I realised that the sexual aspect of crossdressing had long since stopped. I also felt my GI had reclaimed the clothing I felt most comfortable in. Finally, I was dealing with my self-identity.

So, if we are to consider the matter of primary femininity, it is my belief that the development of one's GI formation might not really have a lot to do with identification with the mother. I see that more of an attachment-based issue and not necessarily something for this book to discuss. What I will say is that if boys must dis-identify with their mothers and by default identify with their fathers to ensure that a healthy GI is formed, then I predict problems with this theory. Firstly, not all fathers are present either emotionally or geographically in their son's life. Secondly, who's to say that the father has the correct amount of masculinity (remember we are all on a spectrum) about them to provide a substantial and healthy presentation for the establishment of a male GI? And thirdly, does this theory transfer to all cultures on the planet? To my knowledge, and I admit I am not an anthropologist, not all cultures attribute the same level of value to masculinity and patriarchy as we appear to do in the West. As we saw in Part 1 of this book, there are lots of traditional cultures which have a better understanding of GI and can do GV with less discomfort and more understanding than we do in the West.

I think that it's valid to ask the question: 'Who do these theories of gender development serve?' Does knowing theory mean you are a more effective therapist, or that you are better placed to understand the issues that self-identified GV clients are likely to bring into the session? Will this knowledge and similar theoretical positions improve the day-to-day plight of GV individuals? I can say with confidence that there are very few, if any, GV clients whom I have worked with clinically over the years who would need/want to understand the 'Why/How?' of their GI. This is due to the physical nature of their situation and the fact that they are out there in society attempting to live their lives under confusing and precarious circumstances. They present within our consulting rooms as individuals struggling to achieve a personal meaning of the dialogue, both spoken and sensed, between the experiences of their core-self (internal self) and the experiences of their physical body (external self). How do they go about living their life whilst being in this position and what is it to be in the world? I base this view on many hours of observations in clinical work with GV clients.

The clients' lived phenomena conveyed during therapeutic work include their real, day-to-day exertions of existing as GV people – for example: their struggles of acceptance or rejection by family, friends and even society at large; the strains of accessing help from the oversubscribed medical services; how they manage any mental-health matters brought about by the pressures of the again oversubscribed medical services; and generally attempting to have as meaningful and normal a life as anyone else. Their being in the world is the fundamental substance of the work; without it there is no work.

So, to go back to my initial question: 'Who do these theories of gender development serve?' In my opinion the theories serve the needs of academics, and academics alone. All this is indicative of patriarchal pathologising in relation to the formation and presence of GV, as these theories were predominantly created by men and speak of classifying any deviation from the binary as psychologically abnormal, or as a disease. Essentially, it is the pathologising of GV and proffering an evolutionary model which promotes the binary as natural. Certainly, primary femininity can appear to be merely a nod in the direction to redressing what appears as a massive imbalance created by these patriarchal theories. I feel strongly that a theoretical model can only have a value if its content has a practical application to the client work, and by this I mean that it helps the client to understand the experiences they have of themselves being their self in the world. While I have respect for Freud and those who followed him (I do have space for the unconscious within my client work), I feel that history pays testament to the reasons and conditions behind theoretical models and their honourable intent (i.e. betterment for the individual's quality of life). However, as we have seen throughout this book's narrative, there have been many times throughout history when laws and beliefs – and I think we can include theoretical models here, too, as they are presented in academic tomes as totems for individuals to consider and subscribe to – have been used to impose control over certain parts of society which are considered undesirable or of less value.

Over the many years I have been travelling around the UK delivering training programmes to counsellors, psychotherapists and those who support GV people during their work, time and time again at the end of the training the attendees say that my training programme is 'alive' because I bring real life into it. I don't shy away from telling of the struggles trying to get a GP to take you seriously when you tell them you require help, the frustration with the GI clinics when you're told it will be nearly two years before you can receive your first appointment, the abandonment of friends and family, the gains and the losses which come with being yourself, the understanding of what it can be like to finally feel whole or as whole as is possible to be. I will often have Tina, my long-term partner and now my wife, delivering the trainings with me and this adds another dimension to the overall whole of the GV experience. She is often asked what it is like to be in a relationship with someone who has moved across the gender border and isn't the person you began the relationship with.

When the individual transitions, all those close to them transition as well, because their position in the relationship with their GV loved one forces them to change their relationship (e.g. a son becomes a daughter or vice versa, a husband becomes a wife, etc.). As Julia Serano said, the lives of those who are GV are works of non-fiction. They certainly are not the subjects of academic study which are developed into theories. This is not to say that there aren't certain techniques which can be useful to clinical practitioners in the work with a client exploring their GI, and this we will come to in the next chapter. Before we go there, let's first look at a couple of sociological concepts which I feel do bring something constructive to our exploration.

Essentialism and Constructionism

Essentialism is the view that everything that is present in the world has a set of attributes that are necessary to its identity and function. Philosophically it's been considered that all things have such an essence, idea, form, substance. It is the thing which makes it what it is, and without it, it would not be that thing. So, a simple example of essentialism would be to consider the essence of something like a chair. Now we know from experience that chairs necessitate by their very purpose something to sit upon off the ground. They require legs to perform this task (okay, chairs vary and may have fewer than four legs or no legs at all, but for the sake of the example let's stick with this). The legs then usually connect with a platform, which we place our bottom on, and it will have a back that we can lean against. Regardless of the design of the chair and its unique style and construction, its essence is these three parts:

- legs

- platform to sit on

- back to lean against.

Essentialism has been questioned throughout history and, in some cases, contested in the extreme by saying that if we are going to apply this rule of essence to everything, will this apply to things like dirt, mud and even lint? I certainly don't feel a need to take something which I may not agree with and mock it; I will simply choose not to invest any time on the subject. I do find the unyielding nature of essentialism a touch unhelpful as I feel that as clinical practitioners it is fundamental that we are open to all shades between two poles. In biology and other natural sciences, essentialism has offered the rationale for categorisation or taxonomy, at least until the time of Charles Darwin. The function and importance of essentialism in biology is still debated, and as we saw with the work of Joan Roughgarden, nature doesn't fit nicely into clear definitions.

Gender essentialism is regarded by some feminists as the fixed attribution of essence to women. This essence is assumed to be universal and is generally identified with those characteristics viewed as being specifically feminine. These ideas of femininity encompass both biology and psychological characteristics, including nurture, empathy, support and non-competitiveness. The feminist theorist Elizabeth Grosz takes this thought even further by considering that not only does essentialism define women's essence as being shared by all women always, but that the essence has a limitation within which a woman will define her own personal traits. She goes on to say that the essence has a limitation to which a woman will define her own personal traits within this structure. Also, it is not possible for a woman to act in a manner contrary to her essence, and that her essence underlies all variations differentiating women from one another. Grosz's view ultimately leads us to the position that if this rule applies to femininity, it must also apply to masculinity. This essentialist concept that men and women are fundamentally fixed in their biological, psychological and sociological differences continues to be a matter of contention. Back in 1995 when Grosz made these claims in her book *Space, Time and Perversion: Essays on the Politics of Bodies*, it was a very different world to the one in which I am now writing these words. Advancements/changes in all areas of society's growth, including sex and GI, have meant that a clear distinction of what essentialism states is female and what is male has become less certain. We can no longer assume that physically all men have a penis and no breasts, and that all women have vaginas and breasts. We can no longer make assumptions about male and female sociological traits and roles where men are tough, hard and competitive whereas women are soft and emotional. We are living in a world where a GV man gave birth to a baby, and this throws questions at the universal laws we have lived with until now.

However, there is another structure which we can view reality through, and although constructionism is a concept with fundamental attributes, these can be less rigid and allow for flexibility, growth and change to happen in the lifetime of the subject being examined. Social constructionism or the social construction of reality (social concept) is a theory of knowledge in sociology and communication theory that examines the development of jointly constructed understandings of the world that form the basis for shared assumptions about reality. This can also be known as 'Tulpa' (modern specialists use the term to refer to a type of imaginary individual, whom the practitioners consider to be a sentient/independent being sharing their head space). I see this as the part of us which we may have an inner dialogue with. It is considered part of us, although we have a sense that it is separate; and as we engage in an exchange with this self, we somehow know it's part of us and separate at the same time (it may not physically exist other than as a voice or sounding vacuum). The social constructionism theory centres on the notions that human beings rationalise their experience by creating models of the social world and sharing figures of speech through language. Social constructionism concerns the meaning, notion or connotation placed on an object or event by a society and adopted by the inhabitants of that society with respect to how they view or deal with the object or event. In that respect, social constructionism as an idea would be widely accepted as natural by that society but may or may not represent a reality shared by those outside the society or subculture within that society, and as such may be an invention or pretence of that society. We see this at play in those who staunchly challenge and attack the existence of GV (e.g. the TERFs' reaction to trans women).

A major aspect of social constructionism is to uncover the ways in which individuals and groups participate in the construction of their perceived social reality. It involves looking at the ways social phenomena are developed, institutionalised, known and made into tradition by humans. In 1966, when social constructionism was in the ascendant, the basic principle that underpinned the theory was that people make their social/cultural worlds and at the same time these worlds make them as they live them. Another aspect of the theory was that reality is both revealed and concealed, and created and destroyed by our activities. It's open to change and evolution and is less fixed than the essentialist position. We are making reality every second of our lives, rather than being a place that we can enter and exit at will. We have no choice but to do reality. Being passive and not engaging in anything isn't not doing reality, but rather a reality where the individual is passive and not engaging in activity.

In social constructionist terms, taken-for-granted realities are cultivated from interactions between and among social agents (by agents I include people: groups of people, including sub-groups). The reality is not an objective truth which is waiting to be uncovered through positivist scientific enquiry (by this it means that only science can validate something as being real and that anything which is open to interpretation is excluded). It proposes there can be multiple realities that compete for truth and legitimacy. Social constructionism recognises the value of language and communication, and most social constructionists follow the belief that language does not mirror reality – rather it creates it. And this is evidenced again in the example of the extreme trans activists having their set of beliefs which they choose to subscribe to, and the TERFs having a set of beliefs which they subscribe to, which just so happens to be counter to what the trans activists believe. There is unlikely ever to be an accord reached between these two groups because their respective beliefs are so far removed from one another. If one or other group were to reach an accord, that would demand the other to sacrifice their reality. It is things like this that usually form the basis of conflict as letting go of a belief/reality can feel like a blow to one's very existence.

As we saw in Part 1, historically, the term 'gender' was accepted as a means of distinguishing between biological sex and socialised aspects of femininity and masculinity. Gender was considered to be achieved and stable after being acquired in early childhood. However, the contemporary constructionist perspective, as proposed by American sociologists Sarah Fenstermaker and Candice West (2002), proposes treating gender as an activity 'doing'. These gender activities constitute our belonging to a sex as based on the socially accepted contrast between women and men. It is noted, however, that these activities are not always perceived by the onlooker as being either masculine or feminine, and there is the constant possibility of them being assessed as more or less womanly or manly. However, this isn't such a big risk as in due course any behaviour could be assessed based upon its manly or womanly character. The doing of gender is in fact founded on the interplay which is constituted as ongoing assessments in various situations. This emphasises the situational nature of gender rather than an inherent essentialist characteristic. As we saw when we looked at essentialist theory, gender normalities are often constructed by co-existing features and needs. Social constructs of binary gender models are usually predestined and not given a choice in how they present their version of that identity within this category. And this becomes an important aspect for us as we as a species have a great need to label a person. It becomes a priority, for example, when getting to know one another based on looks, and the way someone portrays themselves is how we categorise them. In those moments we are relying on gender stereotypes to give us a head start in that fact-finding process.

Feminist psychologist Lisa Diamond and co-writer Molly Butterworth address this matter in the chapter titled 'Trans-gender Experience and Identity' of the 2014 book *The Handbook of Identity Theory and Research.* They describe how GI and sexual identity are fluid and do not always fall into two essentialist categories (man or woman, and gay or straight) through their interviews with sexual minority women over the course of ten years. They provided a case study of one woman who had a seemingly normal/stable childhood, yet around adolescence began questioning her sexuality but remained stable in her gender and sexual identity. She began working with men and adopted a masculine position and began questioning her GI. She later transitioned to a male and began to find men attractive and moved towards identifying as homosexual.

In much the same way we stereotype gender to label one another, we also have these stereotypes when it comes to sexuality. Heterosexuality is assumed to carry certain characteristics of the men and women involved for those individuals who appear to act appropriately masculine or appropriately feminine. If one wants to be perceived as a lesbian, one must first be perceived as a woman; if one wants to be a gay man, one must be seen to be a man. However, there is more to this than the individual visual presentation. What is often overlooked in relation to GI is that it's much more than what you look like regardless of sex. More importantly it's the 'doing' and the 'how' of the 'doing' which constitutes your gender in a world that considers a person is not simply what one is, but what one does. Everything you do in every minute of every day, both consciously and unconsciously, is you 'doing' your gender. It is for everyone to come to realise and acknowledge that what and who we are is a constant ebb and flow of expression of our core GI. The creating of gender is usually accomplished alone. However, it can also be accomplished around/with others, and even in the imagined presence of others. Some gender theorists will say that doing gender is not just about conforming to stereotypical gender roles but is also the active engagement in any behaviour that is regarded as gendered. My issue with this statement is that they appear to be placing too much emphasis on there being some behaviours which are male and some that are female. Despite this, I do of course agree to some extent in that binary behaviours normalise the essentialism of sex categories. In other words, by doing gender, we reinforce the essential categories of gender – for many there are only two categories that are mutually exclusive. The very idea that men and women are essentially different is what makes men and women behave in ways that appear essentially different. This is something which I will challenge later in the book. So now let's look at an influence which we have not considered so far in our journey in understanding GI.

Core Gender Identity

As we have seen, gender constructionism emphasises that one's sense of GI is acquired through the internalisation of external phenomena. Following this principle, we acknowledge that we are never fully developed and as such we are a work in progress, due to our ongoing exposure to external phenomena.

However, defining GI is not as straightforward as whether we approach it from constructionist or essentialist methodologies. Why? Because there is a fundamental factor which we have not taken into full consideration, which is that every one of us has a core GI. Obviously, we don't consciously know this, but it gives us hints and nudges as to its presence and its definition. We will look at this in more detail later, but now I want to introduce you to the American psychologist Carl Rogers, who was one of the founders of the humanistic therapeutic or what he called 'client-centred psychology'. He considered that within all of us there is what he called the 'organismic self' and this is best defined as our innate and true self. The organismic self is sometimes referred to as the 'real self', describing the real self as 'that part of one's identity felt or considered to be authentic'. The term implies that there is a quality of authenticity beneath the persona/public self that we present to the world. Thus, the organismic self is the true self; it is there when we are born, and it naturally strives towards growth, maturity and self-actualisation, which would happen if we were allowed to grow and flourish without external factors impacting upon us. The organismic self knows what it needs both from its environment and from other people, i.e. our relationships, to be able to actualise, to achieve a realisation and attainment of our potentialities. Although the organismic self is present at birth, the expression of positive regard towards us by significant people in our life can become more significant than our own organismic valuing process, and we begin seeking positive regard from others at the expense of achieving our true self.

This process of taking on conditions of worth (CoW) often continues without the child being aware of it, meaning that we end up as adults who quite naturally experience incongruence between who we are and who we feel we should be. Our core GI is a facet of this organismic self. It is the blueprint of the true and authentic part of who we are, and how we naturally want to present our self in the world. It has at its core a fixed and consistent nature which remains throughout the course of our life. I often see this as a homing beacon pulsing out our true essence. This essence is subtle and requires us to listen to ourselves carefully, because the noise of the world can easily drown it out. As I mentioned in the Introduction, very often the core GI essence is experienced in fleeting glimpses which are never fully quite grasped or understood in the moment. It's usually not until a lot later, when the individual has begun to engage and explore the essence, that they have a stronger sense that it's their GI which is speaking to them and that they have begun a process of exploration of their GI. It is possibly then that the individual might experience an overwhelming sense of distress between the internal and external worlds, and this is when they are likely to experience gender dysphoria.

I want to address the point that some may look at this model and say that our core GI cannot be fixed because we may feel that our true nature or self evolves and changes during our lifetime. However, I see this more as the result of how we come to view our observation of this process of exploration. We view our internal self from the location of the external world with its constant in-flow of transitory external phenomena. This process is ongoing and is why we are a work in progress. Because we are continually exposed to and experience life phenomena, it makes the process of discerning our true core GI harder because we are continually sifting for things which resonate with our core GI, while disregarding the things which don't fit. We could look at this process as being like trying to tune into the beacon through static interference. We get traces of the signal and then it can become lost, only to be picked up again at a future time. Another factor we must be mindful of is that we will constantly be at risk of being pulled away from the beacon's signal, due to the continued exposure of CoW (see Chapter 6) and the detrimental effects which I have mentioned previously. Sometimes the conditions will present unconsciously, with societal conditioning about what is acceptable/unacceptable. At other times it will be very clear what will happen if we transgress them, such as friends or loved ones telling us how to behave or what they expect of us.

The final factor at play here is how our physical lives impact and regulate us in aligning the orientation of our external world and our internal core GI. We have already looked at how we perceive the number of phenomena we are exposed to daily, and how that requires processing, but then what happens when we find something that fits us, and we want to begin living it? Again, a major factor here will be the CoW, and now we are going to be tested. Say, for argument's sake, we have decided that as a biological male I want to begin openly wearing nail varnish. I know that the implicit rules of Western society say that this behaviour is not usually permitted for men, so I have a choice: do I continue abiding by the rules of society and negate my true self, or do I align my external and internal selves and wear the nail varnish? We know that transgressing the rules will mean some level of difficulty and questioning by those I encounter in my life. Part of how I decide which path to take will be based upon how secure I will feel by choosing to go down the route of personal authenticity and how I will deal with those who challenge me because of my 'transgression'. An important point to note here is that when we hear of someone transitioning we often wrongly assume that this takes place in one go on one day and that transitioning applies to all areas of the individual's life. For some this may be the case, but for others it can be a process of coming out to certain people whom they feel safe to disclose to, and then over time widening this group of people. Coming out and transitioning are also governed by other factors in the individual's life; for example, do they feel they would be able to come out within their workplace or school/college? Also, finances will also have some bearing on how the individual transitions and comes out, as certain aspects of transition are the responsibility of the individual to finance (e.g. body hair removal or certain surgical procedures which might be required to ensure a better quality of transitioned life). Depending on where the individual lives in the world, there may be factors for them to be mindful of before making the step of transitioning; for example, internal conflicts involving religious beliefs, upbringing and internalised transphobia, in addition to feelings of fear and isolation. Also, there are potential negative social, legal and economic consequences such as disputes with family and peers, job discrimination, financial losses, violence, blackmail, legal actions, criminalisation and, in some countries, even capital punishment. So, this step is not one to be taken lightly.

'In the Region of'

GI is so much more than a social consensus or something which is theorised for any purpose other than to aid a client's understanding. It is the way real people experience themselves within their lives and express their independence of what is for them being male, female or other. And as we have seen, this is their process of sensing what their organismic self is communicating to them. This allows much more space for describing their unique variations (i.e. their core GI).

Returning to the consideration that gender is a doing activity and one that is not static, we have seen already how it evolves for an individual. We are reminded of the quote by Simone de Beauvoir: 'One is not born a woman, but becomes one' (de Beauvoir 2011, p.283). She is suggesting the notion that womanhood or femininity is accomplished through an active process of creating gender through interacting with others in a social context. If we are to accept de Beauvoir's quote (which I think is by and large on the right track, although maybe it is not far reaching enough in allowing for an active process of doing gender, much as I described earlier as a sifting of experienced phenomena), we must therefore accept that this process must also apply to how men 'become'. But I would like to go a bit further and return to my quote from the end to the introduction to the book where I expanded de Beauvoir's quote to represent all gender identities: 'One isn't born, but rather becomes one's gender identity.' The male and female are far from satisfactory classifications; however, they can only exist as part of a spectrum of GI, and we should be reminded that, as with any classification on the spectrum, what is determined is a localisation of that GI for any given individual's presentation. So, we could say that a person who presents their GI as a male is in the region of a masculine man, or a female is in the region of a feminine woman. This might be as close as anyone can be to being a man or a woman.

With this in mind, what would we find on the gender continuum if we applied the idea that any GI is merely 'in the region of'? Let's adjust our understanding of the gender binary of male and female with: 'I am a male in the region of a feminine man.' Or: 'I am a female in the region of a masculine woman.' We can now see that the binary has some shades of tonality and is less black and white than it is usually regarded as being. Let's explore this further by now incorporating the aspect of GV: 'I am a GV person in the region of a feminine transsexual woman.' Or: 'I am a GV person in the region of a masculine transsexual man.' Again, further tonalities have become apparent, and suddenly

GI becomes nuanced and characterised with subtle shades of meaning and expression. Taking this further still, let's see what happens: 'I am GV in the region of a masculine transsexual woman.' Or: 'I am GV in the region of a feminine transsexual man.' This apparently simple process now opens the range of GIs that can exist for us. However, only with further and specific exploration might we be able to investigate the variations that will exist within the population of planet Earth. In the next chapter we will explore the skills and techniques which will aid this therapeutic enquiry and deepen our understanding of the variations of gender. As we go into the next chapter I would ask you to hold in your mind the discoveries we have made in this chapter regarding the broadness of intersex within society and how GV is a personal regional understanding.

EXERCISE 4: PERSONAL MEANING – PART 2

In the next chapter we are going to explore how our clients might begin making sense of how they experience their GI, how they come to understand these feelings/thoughts and how these are translated into the physical world. So, to get you thinking about this process, I am going to present you with the following thoughts.

Our identity: How do we know who we are?

We are who we are... And for the most part we accept that. We may not like certain parts of ourselves; however, we know, understand and accept that they are part of us. The same applies to the parts we recognise as aspects we enjoy or like about ourselves. Both facets are carried with us over the course of our life. Sometimes they change, yet overall they are consistent in their presentation as part of us. So, another question I would like to offer for your consideration is:

How do you know what makes you...you?

I would like to invite you to please take a few minutes to think about and reflect upon this. I think that the core of what I'm asking you to consider is: 'What informs your knowledge of who you are?' It's important to clarify that what I'm asking here is not about knowing about your likes and dislikes – these are easier to figure out, and they are not the things I am asking you to contemplate. I'm asking you to see if you can peel back a few layers of your inner self and ask as a means of a starting position:

How do you know you are the sexuality you are?

Okay, now you have attempted the above, I would like you to reflect on:

How do you know you're the gender you experience yourself as?

How can you be sure of anything you believe/d or sense/d about yourself?

Make some notes and keep them to hand for Chapter 9.

In Treatment 3: Excerpts from my Phenomenological Therapy Journal

It's late in the year 2011 and we are about to join Mark at what will be the next significant point in his life. However, before we look at what is happening, I think it might be useful to catch up with events leading up to this time. Two years previously, Mark undertook a self-detox from alcohol. Many factors had been building over the years leading to his problem with alcohol dependence, yet one of the most significant factors compounding the alcohol addiction was his dissonance around his GI. Episodes of gender dysphoria were daily occurrences now, and Mark was struggling with experiencing it on occasion several times a day. In addition to this, he was working and living in London and was exhausted and burning himself out. During the previous year he'd worked hard within therapy with his therapist Sanja to acknowledge the alcohol dependence to himself and those around him who needed to know, and then to prepare the way to undertake the detox. By October 2008 Mark had assembled himself a comprehensive support network for the task at hand. Equipped with chlordiazepoxide (Librium) prescribed by the GP, twice-weekly support from a north London alcohol service which provided him with key working and acupuncture, and twice-weekly sessions with his therapist, he was as ready as he was ever going to be in addressing what was ahead of him. He would supplement his support by attending AA sessions where necessary.

He had acknowledged to himself that he had created this problem for himself and this was something that, despite all the support in place, only he could change. So, it was on a late October evening, with the daylight shortened by the clocks going back, and rain mizzling in the air, that he found himself stepping out of Belsize Park tube station and walking up Haverstock Hill, with the shinning wet pavement dazzling his eyes due to the cars' headlights. He took the short walk to the Premier Inn. He smiled to himself when he checked in, thinking that Lenny Henry, who fronted the adverts for the hotel chain, had overlooked its full range of functions. Mark swallowed his laughter as he signed in, imagining Lenny saying, 'Premier Inn for all your alcohol detox needs!'

Later that same evening Mark stood in the bathroom on his own, cold sober for the first time in longer than he cared to remember and prepared to take the first dose of chlordiazepoxide. He thought with a sense of irony how many people checked into impersonal hotels, motels and inns around the world to disappear and possibly end their lives in a bleak and muffled anonymity. And here he was, looking for some isolation, not to obliterate his mind and feelings but to do the opposite, so he could begin to feel emotions and begin listening to that subtle essence and to effectively reclaim his life from the substances which had ceased being helpful all those years ago and now were preventing him from becoming.

There was a positive outcome as Mark managed to take control of his substance misuse. He went on to turn the focus of his therapy into dealing with the dysphoria, which without the alcohol was experienced in a fuller intensity than before.

So, back to 2011. Mark is now living in Peterborough with long-term best friend and soon-to-be partner and future wife, Tina. Tina was the first person to nurture Mark's GI and, with her, Mark has begun to slowly and steadily allow the inner essence to manifest in the outside world.

Mark is working with an integrative therapist called Philip. What is important for Mark is that Philip has experience of working with GV, and this is essential as events are drawing to a culmination.

PHILIP: So how did that phone call with your mother go?

MARK: Not so good. Well, not so bad, but possibly not so good, depending on how you view things. I think I might have inadvertently outed myself to her.

PHILIP: What do you mean?

MARK: Tina and I are possibly meant to be going down to visit in a few weeks and Mum asked me if when I next come to visit I wear my 'proper clothes'.

PHILIP: Proper clothes? What proper clothes?

MARK: Well, exactly. It's quite clear she is acknowledging that my wardrobe now includes many items which she feels uncomfortable with. These items are female in nature, and added to that I'm wearing make-up. But that's been happening for the last 18 months now.

PHILIP: So what did you say when she said about wearing your proper clothes?

MARK: I was straight with her and said that these are my day-to-day clothes and that there isn't another wardrobe option.

PHILIP: And what was her response to that?

MARK: She went quiet and didn't know what to say. I got the feeling that she wasn't totally surprised that I said something like this, but I guess she hadn't figured out what to say in reply because that would be taking things into a very uncomfortable place and having to acknowledge there was something going on. You know they are very adept at burying their heads in the sand for as long as possible when faced with anything remotely challenging or unknown.

PHILIP: So how do you feel about this reaction?

MARK: Like how I always feel when they and I end up touching on an emotive issue. Fucked off because it feels again we're headed into an emotional cul-de-sac because this, like everything before it, won't go anywhere because if it's something from outside the realms of known it is automatically seen as a threat! I've told you how they couldn't handle my previous mental health difficulties, yes? Oh, and not to mention my alcohol detox — more shame for them to come to terms with. I feel I must be such a fucking let-down to them.

PHILIP: Okay, so what do you perceive the threat is as you understand it?

MARK: We can only guess, can't we? It's not like we will know for sure.

PHILIP: Yes, of course, but what is your feeling in relation to how this has gone so far?

MARK: The thing which strikes me is that they have seen how much I've struggled in life: mental health, drinking, giving up drinking, and contending with a life beyond alcohol, and finding happiness in my life. You know that is something they always said to us: 'We just want you to be happy.' Well, I'm closer to that than I have ever been before, and I know the region of this happiness.

And just because I choose to wear the clothes that I do doesn't make me a bad or wrong person does it?

PHILIP: No, it doesn't, but I wonder if they are possibly anticipating what wearing the clothes you do might mean? What might be coming next? You said that you got the feeling your mother didn't sound totally surprised by what you said to her?

MARK: Yes, sure. But her tone sounded disapproving. So, for me it feels as if my happiness is conditional. 'We want you to be happy. However, it can only be in ways which we can understand!' It kinda feels as if they found it easier to accept me when I was unhappy. You don't get that luxury when you have children. You cannot know or expect them to grow up exactly as you would want them to be. It's not like I'm doing anything illegal or going out of my way to hurt anyone.

PHILIP: Sure. I'm wondering where you are at in terms of progression or whatever that might be for you?

MARK: Well, I'm currently waiting for an appointment from the local CMHT [Community Mental Health Team]. I've requested to be seen out of area because I don't want to risk being seen by colleagues. But I'm pursuing a referral to the GIC [Gender Identity Clinic]. I don't know for sure where I'm going with all this. I certainly am keen to begin hormones, but beyond that I don't know yet. I'm sure to figure it out as I go.

PHILIP: Sure, but I meant in relation to your day-to-day presentation?

MARK: I want to be living full-time in the way which feels authentic, a natural me. The more I allow femininity into my day-to-day presentation, it lessens my gender dysphoria. I'm not suggesting that this is a cure-all but it is an instinctive movement onwards from where I am now. From what I have researched, and hopefully understood, if I present at the GIC and have already started the Real Life Test I will be in a good position to be prescribed hormones once I've had the second assessment with them.

PHILIP: Okay, so you want to begin living full-time. Do you think you are ready for that step?

MARK: After this issue of clothing with my mother, I think that there is very little now to stop me. Obviously, there is more to this than merely the wearing of clothes from the supposed opposite sex, but I feel that I'm not doing anything unusual or wrong. I am myself either way but a happier me when I align my inner and outer selves. If I can begin living in the region of feminine, then that is a positive. Plus, there is the hope that the dysphoria will lessen and stop if I transition.

The way I see things is that I know I will never be a biological woman, and whatever I do in terms of bodily alterations confirms that. Whilst that recognition is incredibly hard to feel, there is however a sense of comfort for me knowing that there isn't a physical solution and the problem isn't I am not able to access a cure because there isn't one, so on this I'm reconciled. However, having lived with this part of me in some conscious way for the length of time I have, and how I've come to experience the difficult and painful feelings which occur when I have a dysphoric episode, they are kinda telling me that this doesn't have to be this way and that if I step over the gender border I might find that the mental/emotional discomfort becomes lessened.

That step over the gender border will align my inner and outer selves and that feels like a relief and very positive. There are some who know my intentions who think I'm brave. I don't see this as brave or courageous; it is something which must happen. It feels like all the while this part of me is ignored, I am going to be constantly playing catch-up with myself.

I have some hope that if I present what I am doing in as positive light as possible, then it might be easier for my folks to accept, or at least be happy for me.

PHILIP: It sounds as if you have a pretty good grasp of things. So, on a practical and physical level, other than your family, what else is there that will need preparation?

MARK: My employer will need to know as that will involve some preparation time due to my clients needing to be told and providing them time to get used to the idea and figuring out any sticking points that they may have or answering questions this might raise. Other than that, I don't see any major things.

PHILIP: Okay, that sounds all pretty thought through. You said something a moment ago about living in the region of feminine. What does that mean?'

MARK: It means that for me my current gender presentation is out of alignment with my inner sense of my gender essence. For me my gender essence is closer to that of feminine, and therefore if I align the gender presentation as close as I can to (or in the region of) my gender essence, it is likely that I am going to feel less emotional distress (i.e. dysphoria) and equally there is a chance I'm going to be happier with the way I look.

From what I have been reading, when you begin factoring in all aspects of ourselves endocrinologically, our socialisation and other things as well, I think it is safe to say we are all in the region of the gender we present ourselves to be. I think it comes down to more of a case of how happy we are with that region of gender, and the individual will sense that by what they experience between their internal essence and their external presentation.

PHILIP: So, when you refer to a feminine essence and living in the region of, how do you experience that? What does that mean to you?

MARK: On a very basic level it means that I don't identify with the expectations of what it is to live by the convention of being male within this culture. I look at my male contemporaries, and what seems to drive or motivate them feels lost on me. I am individual, and although I was born with a male body there was always a sense that there was something more to me than the male physical self. I describe it as an internal essence, something drawing my attention to it, reminding me that it is there within me. It doesn't have a name or a shape, but it called for me to experience things which resonate its essence, its energy, its region. It just so happened to be that the things it drew my awareness to happened to be female or feminine: clothes, emotions, behaviours, life stages and experiences – all in the region of feminine.

Masculinity felt lost on me as if I was missing its character, that it was a language which I didn't speak or comprehend. By contrast, feminine was so very the opposite. It made sense, it felt right, it was the right fit, and because my physical biological body was in a male presentation, it didn't mean or make it wrong. In my experience it feels like a lie when cis people say that your physical body determines your gender and we need to accept. Having lived 39 years with the discord created by the experience of GI, I finally knew I didn't have to accept this discomfort any longer and I could make a choice about how I lived my life.

And so, it would be that Mark transitioned and began living full-time the following April, 2012. He did as he said and arranged with his employer time to prepare his clients and gave them a few weeks to get used to the idea and to ask any questions they might have. On Maundy Thursday, Mark left employment for the last time in his life. Over the Easter weekend he also left his life, and Madison stepped into the space that he left. During that weekend, as Madison prepared herself for the task of fulfilling the life which she had needed for so long and now had responsibility for, she felt a tinge of sadness that Mark had struggled so much with the world and just living, and she felt protective and a big responsibility for the gift he had provided and given to her. She promised him that she would do the best of living her life and that she valued everything he had put in place for her so she would have the best chance of making this process as much of a success as she was able to. She also hoped that mark had finally found some peace.

CHAPTER 6

PERSON-CENTRED THEORY AND GENDER ACTUALISATION (ACKNOWLEDGING OUR ESSENCE)

The lies a society will tell itself in order to force people to identify themselves very narrowly and shallowly, and what a struggle it is to burst through those lies and to shove them to one side and to stand up and to start to be your true difficult, contradictory bloody self.

(Clarke 1974)

In this chapter I will be discussing a therapeutic model in general terms, but will come to apply the theory back to GI. Within social animal groups there is always a balance to be struck between the needs of the individual and the needs of the group. Some animals which live in communities (e.g. ants and bees) have little individual consciousness and exist with what is regarded as a hive mind or a collective consciousness. There is little or no conflict between the individual and the group. Yet with social animals there is more likelihood of conflict between the individual's needs and those of the group. Wolves, lions, etc. all operate in these kinds of social groupings, and it is for the individual to learn to curtail and control their individualism so that they are accepted and fit into the group. The individual will need to weigh up the costs versus the benefits of belonging to a group. This was true for the hunter-gatherers (whom we spoke of in Chapter 2); nevertheless, they still enjoyed a huge amount of individual freedom, much like other social animals. This all markedly changed for humans with the adoption of agriculture and the beginnings of domestication, and was transformed further with the occurrence of the fall and the beginnings of modern civilisation.

For us to fit into our civilisation currently, we have come to suppress our individuality and curtail our freedoms to a degree which is unprecedented in the previous hundreds of thousands of years of human history. Yes, we may believe we have certain freedoms and the space to express ourselves as we wish; however, there are still unspoken rules at play which we transgress at our peril. Domestication has brought with it many benefits (e.g. healthcare, homes to live in, foods of all varieties, cars, computers, etc.); yet this profusion which comes from being part of society carries a cost to the individual. With poor mental health, unemployment and poverty reaching higher levels than they have been at in many years, employers demanding more of their employees with little or no recent pay increase, and hatred of difference triggering hostility within parts of society, we have come to depend on laws to protect us against discrimination (protected characteristics) and to uphold the fair and equal treatment of people. Under these conditions, we as a society have all had to learn to balance some of our seemingly less accepted aspects of our selves so that other personal needs can be met. We have all learned the need to do this within the first tribe we encounter in life – our family. To ensure our basic needs are met we might change our behaviour or live in ways in which we split off or deny certain aspects of our fundamental selves, thus enabling us to fit in and be accepted. This way of learning continues throughout our lives as we mature, grow and go out into the world, but at what personal cost to ourselves? It's very often this cost which leads people to enter into therapy as the void between who they are and how they present themselves to the world begins to cause personal discomfort. Let us now turn our attention to the model of therapy I wish to focus upon.

The American psychologist Carl Rogers was among the founders of the humanistic, or person-centred, approach to psychology. The main principle of this approach places emphasis on the individual/client accepting responsibility for their own life and trusting their inner resources. The theory suggests we all have these inner resources available to us if we are prepared to set out along the path of self-awareness and self-acceptance.

The person-centred model places at its core that people become cut off from their essential resources and divorced from their fundamental ability to make judgements about their existence – what Rogers called the 'Organismic Valuing Process' (OVP) (Mearns and Thorne 1988). Rogers believed that through the OVP a person has a sense of what they need for their enrichment in the world. The problem we all face, as above, is that we as intelligent social animals feel the need to fit into whatever social groups we have in our lives (e.g. family, friends, school, etc.). This raises issues of approval and the receiving of positive regard, as we also acknowledged earlier. Rogers called this 'conditions of worth' (CoW) (Mearns and Thorne 1988), the process of balancing that the individual makes between social acceptance and being their authentic self. These perceived conditions must be met in order for other people to accept us and include us in the group, yet the conditions hamper the maturation of our authentic sense of self. As children, we learn that there are certain things that we must do to be accepted, and other things we must not do. In doing so, we learn 'introjects' (Mearns and Thorne 1988). Introjects are the 'should' and 'should nots', 'oughts' and 'ought nots', 'musts' and 'must nots'. The values get presented to us from an early age from parents, school, religion, advertising and society as a whole. The more complex the society is, the more rules there are, and the more introjects are needed to keep people in line. Once a self-concept has become internalised, the individual is inclined to reinforce it. In essence, what we end up living reflects how we value ourselves; so if we have concluded that we are inept, worthless and unacceptable, then it's more than likely that we will behave in a way which expresses this about ourselves. This usually means that the chances of gaining the approval we seek diminish over time. For some people this possibility of rejection can be interpreted as totally overwhelming, leaving them with only the faintest sense of self-esteem. The individual continually struggles to seek approval while painstakingly avoiding and checking against thoughts, feelings and events which they sense will bring unfavourable outcomes for them.

They have come to truly believe that their sense of worth is conditional on gaining the approval/avoiding the disapproval of those who are important to them, and therefore they censor their behaviour accordingly. They have fallen foul of the CoW of others, and so immense is their need for approval that they accept the conditioning rather than risking rejection. And yet throughout their life, from time to time they may encounter some small trace of something else existing within them, an essence of something so subtle it might be missed if they weren't aware it was part of them. This essence is slight and fleeting, yet despite this, it is unyielding in its reoccurring nature, continually speaking its existence. This is the trace of the OVP offering something more wholesome. It speaks the individual's truth and is the beacon calling out to us when we have become knocked off course by life's conditioning.

The constricted pressure exerted by the CoW becomes more overwhelming over time in that it takes precedence over the OVP, which provides constant encouragement to ensure the individual is never perturbed by the displeasure and anger of a parent or significant person whose approval is vital to the individual's overall well-being. When the individual experiences the OVP, the reaction is likely to be confusion, and if this happens repeatedly it is likely that they will develop a 'Self-Concept' (SC) (Mearns and Thorne 1988), a version of the self constructed from the beliefs one holds about oneself and the responses of others. It is largely a reflection of the reactions of others towards the individual, which serves to continue distancing the self from the OVP or to alienate oneself from, and be distrustful of, it. Repeated distrust can result in the SC blotting out the efforts of the OVP, and with this the individual can ultimately believe what the SC is telling them. If we are regularly told we are bad or unlovable for showing anger, crying, being assertive, saying how we feel, and so on, then we will generally learn to monitor ourselves. We learn to turn a 'condition of worth' into a 'condition of self-worth'; for example, we may change 'You are unlovable because you're emotional' into 'The emotional part of me is unlovable'. Once the SC has brought this unfavourable process to the stage where the individual has become distrustful of their ability to believe in their own capability in decision-making, they seek guidance from outside of themselves: the 'External Locus of Evaluation' (ELoE) (Mearns and Thorne 1988). Rogers believed that a 'fully functioning' person has his or her own source of personal wisdom already (Mearns and Thorne 1988). So, all is not lost, as at our innermost depths we all have a longing and the resources, that are what Rogers referred to as the 'Actualising Tendency' (AT) (Mearns and Thorne 1988). He described it as an inherent tendency within ourselves to grow and reach our full potential. The AT manifests directly through the OVP, which is always trying to direct us to strive and make the very best of our existence and develop to our full potential. One of the important challenges of person-centred therapy is to facilitate through the therapeutic relationship the conditions for the client to begin making a shift from the 'External Locus of

Evaluation' to an 'Internal Locus of Evaluation' (ILoE) (Mearns and Thorne 1988), where the individual can trust themselves to have the answers they need and commence the reversal of the process brought about by the CoW. The client begins to trust in the therapist, and through the healthy relationship they can start to listen without fear, judgement or shame to their OVP.

What of Our Gendered Selves?

Let us now apply this model to the specific matter of our natural gendered self. I will apply it directly to my own experience, going back to one of my earliest experiences which occurred during my explorations into cross-gender dressing and which I highlighted in the first 'In Treatment'. Mark told his therapist, Gina, that he felt awful because he had tried to understand why he crossdressed and, lacking any real options to educate himself, found a book on psychiatric mental disorders in the local library:

> **Mark:** …the book I read in the library said that people who do this are mentally ill and must be treated to stop them doing it. It said we are sexual perverts.

> **Gina:** Well, I don't agree with what the book says, and I think it could help you for if we explore what it must be like for you to experience the crossdressing.

We see several points nicely illustrated here. Firstly, we can see Mark experiencing a negative reaction to his behaviour (i.e. crossdressing is wrong and needs changing). He has taken on the belief that crossdressing is a paraphilia and that those engaging in it require psychiatric treatment to remove this behaviour and return them to normal behaviours that fit with their sex; and he has even incorporated it as part of his self-concept. He has kept this secret to himself for many years and made it his truth. It is not something that he has felt safe to share, as he fully expects that disclosure would run the risk of rejection, judgement and shame.

This brings us nicely to the second point, which is Gina's response. She doesn't meet Mark's expectations of rejection. On the contrary, she not only continues to be accepting of him, despite this additional damning information, but she also carefully but actively challenges the substance of his self-concept (i.e. that those who crossdress are mentally ill). By saying she doesn't agree with what the book says, she is directly challenging this external authority which Mark has taken as law and hurt himself with. Finally, she has modelled for Mark what it's like to trust one's OVP and to be informed by one's ILoE. This is a huge step for Mark because he has now had an experience which is in direct opposition to everything he had come to believe. And while it won't have radically changed his circumstances, he now has a direct experience which says things might be different. By the time of the second 'In Treatment' we can see that some major changes have occurred for Mark. Let's look at another excerpt:

> **Elke:** So, what do you take this to mean? That you wish to be a woman?
>
> **Mark:** I think that if I could have choice over male or female, I would have chosen female, but as that isn't an option it's kinda pointless and the outlook feels very bleak.
>
> **Elke:** No, I understand that. But what about living as a female?
>
> **Mark:** That seems impossible, and I don't even believe I look realistic as a woman!
>
> **Elke:** You're describing there being something other than the desire to wear female clothes, yes?
>
> **Mark:** Yes, the feelings I have told you about seem to be getting worse and it doesn't seem to help when I do crossdress. At times, it feels as if this isn't the version of my life that I was supposed to have.

Elke: But Mark, c'mon. You know there are many people out there who have lived gendered lives other than the one with which they were born.

Mark: What? Do you mean transsexuals?

Elke: Yes.

Mark: Well, I'm not one of them.

Elke: Okay. How is it you are so very sure of this?

The first thing that is noticeable is that Mark's self-concept appears to have become less rigid and judgemental by the very fact that he is able to have a conversation about this subject without the huge amounts of self-criticism and guilt that we saw in the first episode of therapy. He is not only able to talk quite freely about what his GI means to him, he is more accommodating of how he does gender and is even able to acknowledge that if given a choice he would prefer to be biologically female. So, we can see some evolution has taken place since the earlier session of therapy. Finally, it is noticeable from these personal shifts that Mark is beginning to observe, and listen to, the essence of his AT, which is guiding him via his OVP. This process is clarification that he is beginning to shift his ELoE to an ILoE. However, knowing what we know now in terms of how things turned out for Mark, we can see he is still being influenced by his self-concept. When Elke encourages him to consider the bigger picture of how some people have tried to resolve their gender dilemma, he has a very strong reaction to the possibility that he might be similar to them or even be transsexual; or if not that, it might be he can establish his gender 'within the region of'. Shortly, we will look at a theoretical approach that would have aided him to explore the feelings he had and to open up and look at his personal meaning of his GI.

But before we do that, let us look at how things have evolved by the time Mark reaches his third phase of therapy:

Philip: Sure. I'm wondering where you are at in terms of progression or whatever that might be for you?

Mark: Well, I'm currently waiting for an appointment from the local CMHT [Community Mental Health Team]. I've requested to be seen out of area because I don't want to risk being seen by colleagues. But I'm pursuing a referral to the GIC [Gender Identity Clinic]. I don't know for sure where I'm going with all this. I certainly am keen to begin hormones, but beyond that I don't know yet. I'm sure to figure it out as I go.

Philip: Sure, but I meant in relation to your day-to-day presentation?

Mark: I want to be living full-time in the way which feels authentic, a natural me. The more I allow femininity into my day-to-day presentation, it lessens my gender dysphoria. I'm not suggesting that this is a cure-all but it is an instinctive movement onwards from where I am now. From what I have researched, and hopefully understood, if I present at the GIC and have already started the Real Life Test I will be in a good position to be prescribed hormones once I've had the second assessment with them.

The most significant step is that Mark is now fully engaging with his AT and is in tune with how his OVP is attempting to guide him to the most positive and fulfilling outcome in the region of his GI. He may be tuned in to the AT, but this doesn't mean he is in possession of all his answers; yet he appears to be okay with this and being led by his instincts: 'I certainly am keen to begin hormones, but beyond that I don't know yet. I'm sure to figure it out as I go.'

Again, we know that Mark is using his ILoE. What we can also see is that Mark has begun to dispel certain generalised beliefs that he was displaying in his second phase of therapy, where he had a strong reaction to the consideration of transsexuality as an outcome he might relate to: 'But I'm pursuing a referral to the GIC [Gender Identity Clinic]' and 'I want to be living full-time in the way which feels authentic, a natural me. The more I allow femininity into my day-to-day presentation, it lessens my gender dysphoria.' Here we see a clear example of him being open to being in the region of his GI.

Mark appears to have educated himself and seems to have found some personal meaning in his identity because he is requesting a referral to the GIC and you don't ask for a referral there unless you are looking into a medical intervention – either hormones or surgery, or both. He is becoming clearer on the state of what he's experiencing in terms of the psychological and emotional distress that he appears to now recognise with his disclosure of seeking relief from gender dysphoria. He has come to a point where he requires outside assistance to reach his version of actualisation. This shows that he is escaping the grip of the SC from which, as we have seen each time we visited him in therapy, he has released himself a little further. What we can acknowledge is that, regardless of what Mark now feels in whether he identifies with being transsexual or not (it is nothing more than an umbrella term), he has pieced together the essences he has understood from the AT and is translating their meaning and allowing them to become a physical language which he is manifesting in his life. The most significant example of this is that he now talks about beginning the 'RLT', which tells us that he has decided he is far enough along the process and has sufficient understanding of himself to be ready and able to cross the gender border and commence living in as feminine a way as is possible for him to achieve. The process of stepping over the border is also known as 'transitioning' and 'living full-time', and more often than not (but not exclusively) it will involve some level of medical intervention from the GIC.

Up until this point Mark was still not out to his family and wasn't living full-time. Also, his employer wasn't aware, and he had pockets of his life where the CoW and the SC were influencing his choices of how to live. However, we must remind ourselves that because of the nature of GV and its emphasis on changes to physical appearance, there are huge implications, especially if the individual decides not only to come out but to begin living publicly full-time. As counsellors and therapists, we hold responsibility and must monitor ourselves to ensure that we don't get caught up with the belief that the only positive outcome for the client is that they transition, or that they transition before they are ready to do so. There are some very real and detrimental implications for the client if they undertake a change before they are ready and/or understand what that might mean for them – they need to be equipped and adept to live with the outcomes. The client's SC is a phenomenon which we need to be actively engaging with, yet it might be keeping the client safe in some aspects of their life. We need to be vigilant with regard to this possibility, and yet be there to support the client when they feel able to free themselves from its grip.

CHAPTER 7

BEGINNING THE PROCESS OF GENDER IDENTITY ENQUIRY

'So what kind of a woman are you?' or 'What kind of a man are you?'

(Webb, training programme)

These seem like quite simple questions to ask a client who has established that they are either a transsexual woman or a transsexual man. However, very often when these questions are asked, there is a silence of uncertainty. It is interesting to note that a GV person may have a strong sense that something within them doesn't feel right with their GI, yet when asked about an essential and core part of their experience of self, very often they are unable to convey this. So, what can we do as therapists when a client presents as knowing they are something outside the binary yet not clear in what that actually means? As counsellors/ psychotherapists working with GV clients, personal meaning really is fundamental to understanding a client's experience of themselves being in the world and the resulting perception of the self. I see this as a direct route to enable the client to establish their 'in the region of'. This is the beginning of a process which focuses the client to convey their phenomena and develop a picture of what it is like for them by describing the relationship between their sensed self and the physical body that they are experiencing dissonance with. To aid us with this task we are going to work with the philosophical model of enquiry called 'phenomenology'.

The acknowledged founder of this philosophical school was the German philosopher Edmund Husserl. Husserl was profoundly concerned with two aspects regarding how we construct our reality. The first is the notion of 'intentionality' as the centre of all cognitive experience (Spinelli 1989). Putting it more simply, intentionality is the most basic act that the mind engages in (i.e. the translating of the raw data it encounters via our senses). The second aspect Husserl was concerned with was the 'Neoma and Noesis foci of intentionality' (Spinelli 1989). These are the things which shape our experience. Simply put, Husserl is saying that the Neoma is 'the what' we are directing our attention towards and focusing on, while the Noesis is 'the how' when we define an object. The initial responsibility of those who first began working with phenomenology was to use it to undertake an exploration of subjective experience. This notion was to uncover how our consciousness imposes itself upon and eclipses 'pure' reality so it can ultimately isolate conscious experience and arrive at a truthful approximation of 'what is'.

But why? Well, we human beings attempt to make sense of our experiences through cognitive processes and we endeavour to ascertain meaning from the world. Conversely, this very process brings up one of the most basic issues that challenge philosophy: What is real? I say it's a basic idea, yet due to its apparent simplicity we could reply by stating that it's what we see around us: for me, a wooden table, my PC, stone ornaments, a wooden screen; looking farther, I see my garden with my partner busily gardening away. I know these various objects are real to me as I have engaged with them many times. I also know that they are independent of my consciousness in that if I ceased to exist I am sure that they would continue to exist; for example, I can go out, and when I return the efforts of my partner's gardening will be evident – they have an existence which is separate to my own and are therefore real. So, what we have just described here is a theory of reality; and due to it being so clearly obvious to us, we don't even regard it as a theory. Reality is reality, yes? It's just how things are: fact. This in turn has led to the postulation of an 'objective reality'. This takes at its core that there are real objects in the world which exist independently of our conscious knowledge and awareness of them. We all have the ability to experience them through our senses, so what we perceive as being out there in the world is actually there; it is objectively real.

The conclusion we are left with claims that, however true reality is, it will remain forever, at the same time both unknown and unknowable to us. What we term 'reality' (i.e. that which is experienced by us as being reality) is inseparably linked to our mental processes in general, and in particular to our innate capacity to form meaning. This is the starting point of the phenomenological enquiry. As I will confirm, the enquiry or method focuses on the phenomena of consciousness in order to clarify their role in the process of meaningful construction, as well as to set them aside or 'bracket' them in order to arrive at a more satisfactory, if still incomplete, comprehension of reality.

In therapeutic terms we can now begin to see that the established meaning is going to be very personal to the client, and that meaning will be an interpreted version of the client's meaning for the therapist. This is okay because phenomenologists say that this interpretational process must be openly acknowledged as part of what we state our version of reality to be and is normal for how we experience reality. It is fair to say that it's impossible to interpret it any closer than 'in the region of' as we determined earlier, but that is okay and to be expected. To argue the case for whose reality is truly real or 'correct' or 'incorrect' is misleading, because the established data or presented phenomena are relative and based upon internal and external variables.

Bringing the matter back to GI, it is essential to consider that phenomenology theories suggest there is a 'correct' interpretation which would presuppose that we had a knowledge of an 'ultimate reality' in any given situation. This leads us to an interesting situation: that there is no accurate definition of what a man or a woman is; we are all suggestions to our respective gender. We could say, 'Who decided the criteria for what a man and a woman are and why weren't we asked?' It is important to remind ourselves that we are likely to have assumed that our experiences are in some way normal and that our perceptive abilities are in some way unquestionable and more in touch with what we have labelled as reality.

Let us have a look at the process that can be introduced into the work with your client. There are three main stages and two further considerations. For a comprehensive exploration of phenomenology, I suggest reading *The Interpreted World: An Introduction to Phenomenological Psychology* (Spinelli 1989). Spinelli's writing style is very accessible and I have found his book invaluable when working with the natural enquiry of how the client experiences themselves in the world.

As you will see, the method refers to 'rules', but these are not to be regarded as exercises that you would formally introduce to your client; rather they are an exploratory framework within which you would structure your dialogue. I would suggest being mindful before applying the method, in that you consider the conditions which the setting you are working within determines. This may sound obvious, but the method itself comes with no formal structure pertaining to application timescales, so this will be something all practitioners will need to establish for themselves prior to starting out. As we know, if you're working in a setting where you have a limited number of sessions, this will mean that you will have to consider the time constraints of how long you can realistically and appropriately apply the method. What might help you with answering this is an understanding of what the client wants to achieve through the work and what kind of information is produced during the course of the enquiry. Finally, I would add that if you are a practitioner working in a setting where there are no time constraints (i.e. you have autonomy over how many sessions are available to the client), then I would still urge you to consider the timescale for which the method is beneficially applied. As we will see, there will be a point where either that particular route of data-gathering has been exhausted or the direction of the work changes, in which case you may begin to apply a new application of the method.

Steps

Step 1: The Rule of Epoché

This advises us to set aside any initial biases/prejudices that we may have of the client. We are asked to also suspend our expectations and assumptions, and in short 'to bracket' these factors temporarily so that we may focus as far as possible on the primary data/phenomena of our experience with the client. The Rule of Epoché urges us to impose openness on the immediate experience so that our understandings may lead us to authentic information. Now this may appear to be something we as practitioners are doing as a matter of course in our clinical work; however, I hope you can begin to see the specific benefit it brings to the work with GV clients, where establishing a personal meaning allows the client to begin defining themselves. To begin to fully comprehend the benefits of this process, I'm going to present you with a case study to illustrate the Phenomenological Method in action.

I'm about to begin the first session with a new client whom I will call Melissa. This is not her real name. We have only spoken on the phone for a few minutes to confirm some practicalities, and she has given me the preliminary information that they crossdress and have done so for many years. She has a varied life outside the home whilst presenting 'en femme'. They have undertaken and still are undertaking various medical/cosmetic procedures. Now I could go, if I allowed myself to, into all sorts of assumptions about where they are in their journey. The first thing I wish to highlight is the recommendation of Epoché to bracket. No matter how many GV people I have worked with, and all the similarities of patterns and pathways that this type of client group share, in this moment the only client that matters is the client sitting in front of me.

The time comes for the session, and Melissa arrives in what is known as 'Bob mode'. This is a term that a lot of older GV people use to refer to presenting in public in male attire. I notice a slight feeling of surprise within me because the way the client presented themselves on the phone sounded like they were quite advanced down the physical transition route. I expected them to be living full-time, and this might have led me to make further assumptions about what they would want to explore within the therapy. I get a hold of my surprise and the associated assumptions and log it; I don't overlook it because it is a phenomenon that has presented within the therapy. There could be any number of reasons why the client has presented this way for the session, yet in that moment I don't want to allow this to overshadow or exclude the chance of other material being presented. It's always a useful reminder that sometimes the reason might not even be related to gender. As you can see, it is quite easy to form an assumption which might contaminate or get in the way of the enquiry. Being realistic, let me say that it is impossible to bracket all prejudices and assumptions; however, we are certainly able to bracket a significant number of them. And those that get through? Well that's okay, but try not to allow them to get in the way of the process naturally unfolding. Now let's move on to the next rule.

Step 2: The Rule of Description

The essence of this rule is: 'Describe, don't explain.' Having opened up the enquiry as far as possible to the possibilities of our immediate experience through the Rule of Epoché, we are now urged to consider not placing another type of limitation on our enquiry by immediately trying to explain, interpret or theorise the material in terms of the subscribed theories within our therapeutic orientation.

This rule asks us to remain initially focused on our immediate and concrete impressions of 'being with the client and hearing their narrative' and to uphold an openness to these experiences. This builds upon description rather than reducing it via theory to an explanation or conjecture. Having set up a clinical process, we don't want to explain away the phenomena of our source material. When we use theories to explain the phenomena experienced, we use models that separate us from our experience, which in fact could further put the enquiry at risk of contaminating our examination. Description keeps things anchored in the concrete of the material experienced. Describing signifies that we are working with the client's personal meaning and this is the real material of our work. It allows us to gain access over time, similar to an archaeologist systematically peeling back layers of personal meaning. Inviting the client to describe their phenomena of experiencing their GI can eventually reveal an expression of their fundamental essence, or a personal meaning to their behaviour which will be of more authentic value to them. This process could be challenged as not being altogether free of explanatory aspects, and as such the rule aspires towards an ideal which cannot be achieved. I disagree and suggest that explanations run along a continuum, with concrete description at one end and academic theorising at the other. As I have said earlier, I am dubious about the true value to the client of an enquiry which is heavily focus-driven by academia.

If we return to Melissa in the initial part of the session, she reiterates all that she has told me over the phone. She goes on to tell me that she has an amazing social life as Melissa and is always out and about with her friends who know and accept her. She is especially excited to tell me that she has the ability to 'pass' (i.e. makes for a convincing female) in public and this is something she is very proud of. I ask her to describe how she experiences the positive passing and she tells me that she has had several advances from men over the years, although she is at pains to tell me that she is heterosexual and has never acted on one of these occasions. She then tells me that she frequently travels abroad whilst presenting as Melissa and that she has been crossdressing from a young age. She describes the various and familiar stages of GV development. She feels she also would love to be Melissa full-time. I ask her to describe what is stopping her, and she tells me that she and her wife have just celebrated their thirtieth wedding anniversary and that her wife would be devastated if she found out there was this deception in her life again (it came to the surface in the fifth year of their marriage when Melissa's wife discovered some women's clothing in their home). As she initially thought that Melissa/Michael was having an affair, Michael told her about his crossdressing. He managed to salvage the marriage by promising to get rid of all feminine clothes and items and saying that it was a phase which was now over (this is a familiar narrative with secondary transsexuals).

However, after some time the urges returned and, despite trying to ignore and overcome them, he eventually gave way to the feelings and began building a female wardrobe and items and returned to a life of dressing outside the home, engaging in the long process of hair removal and beginning to take hormones. I ask which gender clinic they are registered with, and the reply surprises and concerns me: They tell me that they are not, and they have self-funded all the medication and hair removal (no mean feat when you consider most GV women require several hundred hours of hair removal). I follow up my enquiry and check out exactly how she is obtaining hormones, and my concerns are confirmed when Melissa tells me she has found a source online where she has got a good deal. I am concerned to hear this, as 'do-it-yourself', as it's referred to, is not a safe route to go down. Unfortunately, some individuals choose to self-administer their medication, often because available doctors have too little experience in this matter, or no doctor is available in the first place. And there are some cases where the GIC services are not convinced that this is the appropriate way forward at the time. Sometimes GV people choose to self-administer because their doctor will not prescribe hormones without a letter from the patient's gender specialist stating that the patient meets the appropriate criteria for gender dysphoria. In Melissa's case I will hold onto this information for now, even though there is a duty of care. I am recognising 'my need' to say something to the client regarding this but I don't want to break the flow of the client's narrative by intervening at this precise moment as it could knock us off our information-gathering.

What Melissa tells me next turns out to be a significant piece of information, and interrupting would certainly not have been helpful. She goes on to tell me that there are times when, doing all that she does in investing time being Melissa, she feels life is quite futile and meaningless. Melissa goes on to say, 'I remain very content to be Michael and indulge in those activities that are perhaps quite masculine like woodwork, tree logging, stone-walling, excavating with my digger, etc. These activities have been such a feature of my life. Possibly they are a deliberate distraction from my female side.' That is a considerable disclosure and one I'm happy not to miss out in knowing. For now, let's move on to the next rule.

Step 3: The Rule of Horizontalisation, aka the Equalisation Rule

Having gathered our source material via the 'Rule of Description', this third rule urges us to avoid placing any initial hierarchies of significance/importance upon the descriptive material we have sourced. Instead it demands that we treat all material/phenomena, at least initially, as having equal value or significance. This approach allows us to undertake our examination with far less bias regarding what we have gathered from the client. By simply reporting in a descriptive manner what is consciously being experienced, and avoiding making any hierarchical assumptions with regard to the items of description (by saying something is of more importance than something else), we are provided with far more accurate and meaningful material to work with as the process continues to unfold.

As I have pointed out with Melissa, there is a huge amount of information that has been presented and all of it will need attention at some point, but not now. I imagine the work rather like me trying to piece together a jigsaw without knowing what the image is. I therefore cannot place any significance on the individual pieces because they are all important and all have their part to play in determining the overall image.

Before bringing the method back to Melissa, there are a couple of things to consider in terms of timescales. It is worth giving some consideration now to what an appropriate time frame might be for you to work with the method. There is no predetermined fixed point where we are told we have gathered enough sourced material. Indeed, who is to determine what is enough? And when do we feel it's appropriate to begin allowing our theories to have some place in what happens from this point forward? The way I work with clients isn't so much a case of me deciding to switch off the method and move on to using my theoretical approach, because for me the Phenomenological Method is part of my approach. What I do is change down a gear with the method, so it is still actively engaged, but I now create space to bring in other aspects of my integrative clinical process. Now that you have some sense of the method, you can consider the external influences of time constraints affecting your own client work and how you could apply the method. Phenomenologists have acknowledged this concern of timescales and applying the method in what is called the 'Equal Reality Rule'.

Step 4: The Equal Reality Rule

This states that the method can only be applied temporarily; and since it has no pre-determined end-point, all investigations must set a pragmatic limit to its application.

If we return to Melissa, this first session became one of ten sessions where we worked on the material she brought with her. These sessions took place under conditions of private practice. I allowed the 'Rule of Horizontalisation' to have a primary place in the sessions for at least 4–5 sessions. I then stepped down a gear and began introducing my therapeutic knowledge. The reason to make the change at that time was partly informed by the process of us gathering the phenomena; or as Melissa began to see it, telling me about the shape of things acted as a mirror and I could see her becoming more and more distressed because of the discord that was appearing to her about what she was doing and the way she was feeling. So, although I still maintained all the rules running as the means by which I conducted the exploration, it was time to begin ordering the material. In Melissa's case my main concern was the 'do-it-yourself' hormones. This was an incredibly high-risk thing for her to be doing; and although she told me she was purchasing them off the internet, it was the quantity as well as her constant need to try different products that was incredibly concerning. One session, she brought in a holdall and produced 35 different hormone products. I had to hold onto my shock as in some respects I was surprised that Melissa was alive and well as none of this medication was prescribed and her health was not being monitored. A bit of psychoeducation was required, and I provided her with the details of the Gender GP, an NHS GP who prescribes hormones for a charge and then passes the ongoing prescribing over to the individual's regular GP. This is a safer, legal and more expedient option than waiting for hormones to be prescribed via a GIC. She said she would consider this option, but during the time we were working together she didn't tell me she had begun the Gender GP application process.

The next phenomenon which appeared to be causing quite evident distress to Melissa was complex, with several interwoven aspects. It can be summarised as Melissa's wish to keep the truth about her GV from her wife. This topic was made up of the following factors. Firstly, the lie itself was causing distress – leading a double life was exhausting. Melissa's life appeared to be more fun and varied than Michael's, yet there was the contradiction of her feeling that her time as Melissa appeared to be unfulfilling and not going anywhere. Finally, there was Melissa's statement that she was content with her time as Michael and certain male activities. Now any one of these topics is complex on their own, but when you combine them there is a lot of potential stress, so how we come to understand what is going on for Melissa is imperative. Given this clear acknowledgement of male and female aspects of the client, it seemed appropriate to ask a couple of grounding questions. What I try to do is draw the client's attention to consider the part of themselves that is based on their GI, or at least 'in the region of' their GI. This is also really helpful when working with secondary transsexuals. As they have spent a considerable amount of time in their birth sex, it can be helpful to encourage them to engage and reflect on their truer self by asking the question: 'So what kind of woman/man are you?'

In my experience, the question enables the client to reflect upon their inner experience rather than merely the external image. For the GV person, it is their external self which doesn't match the inner feelings. For many their transition focuses on the external/physical aspect, leaving the inner self unspoken and/or overlooked. Bringing their attention back to their inner world can enable the client to see how best they can align the two. I believe it's important for the individual to identify who it is that's about to take the plunge and step out into the outside world. Something that often arises with transsexual women who transition later in life is that they (myself included) feel driven to experience the developmental stage of adolescence which they may have missed. This is harmless enough, but depending on how they express this, it might cause some problems. It usually results in cases of 40-year-olds dressing in the latest teen fashions. Now, I am all for people doing what they feel like (I will let the fashion police make their own minds up!), but if this fashion choice is taken into the outside world it might draw unwanted attention, which could be troublesome. I also think the question 'What kind of woman are you?' puts some distance between self-expression and self-identity. These two terms indicate that there is a vast difference between them, and it is my belief that this is what causes a lot of confusion within the GV population and various sections of society. This is partly why I have chosen to abandon the term 'transgender'. I will pick this point up more fully in the final chapter. I did ask Melissa this question, and with total respect to her she wasn't able to answer it other than from her physical experiences. Shortly after the session where she struggled to answer this question, she ended therapy. I obviously cannot know with any certainty, but I did wonder if she found the work too uncomfortable or she wasn't as ready to explore these matters as she thought she might be.

'What Kind of Woman Am I?'

As I am not able to conclude the case study, I will ask myself the question in order to give you the chance to see how a transsexual woman might answer it.

Firstly, let me clarify that I am a 46-year-old woman. One of the biggest causes of my gender dysphoria was that I never felt I identified with typical Western male culture. The male body I had grown up inside was out of sync with how I felt within; my interests and emotional world had more in common with, but not exclusively to, femininity.

My emotions now seem to be a better fit in the region of femininity (i.e. most of the prominent ones are traditionally softer and compassionate – compared with those of the hegemonic male!). I am a very gentle individual and have worked most of my life in a caring profession. I enjoy culture and the arts and find that a piece of music or art easily elicit an expressive emotional reaction of appreciation. It now feels the reaction makes sense in that my emotions fit better. I used to find I received a lot of negative reactions to my expressions of emotion whilst living in the region of a male child/adolescent; for example, my father asserted that I was a 'drip' and made various attempts to toughen me up. I am spiritual but not religious, and I have found that this path has felt more congruent by approaching it from a female position.

I always had an interest in fashion, but although I'm aware of current trends I rarely follow them – I like to plough my own furrow. I have become a less-is-more girl and wear a basic amount of make-up and have a personal style which I downplay when I am out in public. I have a low-key image which essentially lets me blend in, and that has been my dream – to be an ordinary woman. I acknowledge that even with several years of hormone replacement therapy behind me I still have broader shoulders than I would like and I'm carrying a few pounds more than I'm keen on. My voice is my biggest tell (it being male), and sometimes if I forget myself I still tend to stomp instead of taking smaller steps.

In my answer I have demonstrated that a lot of my inner world, as I experienced it throughout my life, felt distorted both developmentally and socially. My interests nearly always sat within the more feminine areas, as did my emotions. In terms of clothing, as I have said, I always felt frustration that I was socially excluded from certain clothes, styles, textures and fabrics. I'm curious and interested in my look, yet it's also about fitting in and not drawing undue attention to myself, which is what a lot of transsexual women are looking for. I learnt very early on in my life that most of what I experienced of my authentic self and AT appeared to not be allowable within the family and culture which I was brought up in. My SC was established to keep me safe and yet give me a chance to receive the components I required to be acceptable and looked after as a child. It is not often that I make a sweeping statement, but I will do so here because I can say with 100 per cent certainty that this is the case for all GV people.

Assumptions are where some GV individuals are led off the path of personal authenticity, by settling for a 'close as' position, yet very often these individuals end up with a far from satisfactory outcome as they exchange one gender binary for the other. I have come to wonder how many of these individuals have explored the subtleties of their GI. I have experienced this many times with GV clients – they haven't explored themselves fully, and this position can be incredibly harmful as they are not acknowledging the subtler frequencies of their gender range. This confusion frequently shows itself in the therapeutic relationship when I ask transsexual clients: 'What kind of woman or man are you?' The results are often worrying when we consider all that these people are setting themselves up to face and go through. They very often have never given that question a single thought.

Society demands that we all adopt a position with an understandable label, so we all know where we stand and can have a relationship with that label. This being the case, we will get individuals taking positions of 'I'm a trans man/woman', 'I'm a crossdresser', 'I'm genderqueer'. When these individuals self-determine, there is a risk of sticking by what keeps them safe. What does it matter if we end up being a 'free-styling male with feminine tendencies' or a 'gay butch female with overtones of purple essence'?

This takes me back to my initial training 17 years ago, and to what Rogers terms the 'organismic valuing process':

> This fundamental, intrinsic or 'organismic' valuing process helps the person to have a sense of what they need for their enhancement both from the environment and from other people...
>
> ...the need for the positive regard and approval of others can be overwhelming, and not infrequently this need takes precedence over the promptings of the intrinsic valuing process...

> When the organismic valuing process comes into conflict with the need for approval the outcome must be confusion and where this happens repeatedly a person will be forced to develop a self-concept which serves to estrange them almost completely from their organismic experiencing or to make him profoundly distrustful of it. (Mearns and Thorne 1988)

I believe that in the moment when we pass into the world from our mother we have the innate capacity to move towards the fulfilment of our potential. At the deepest level, there is in all of us a yearning and the wherewithal to become who we are, but we get stricken when we enter a prejudiced world – a world that is full of anxiety-ridden people desperately worrying what others think and whether they are acceptable. Trying to stay afloat in a world where our values are decided by faceless politicians and media executives. Falsely believing we are of value and acceptable by the number of friends we have on Facebook or followers on Twitter. Propping ourselves up through CoW, where we choose to behave in ways which are accepted by others and therefore meet with their approval, and yet in that moment another part of our true self falls away.

The Modes of Gendering and Transgendering

I want to conclude this chapter by turning our focus onto physical transformation. For many people considered to be cissexual the physical aspect of GV has always received the most focus in the media. It seems we like being amazed at how the human body can be changed by scientific, medical and cosmetic processes. I believe that even though we currently are unable to defy the body's natural process of ageing and dying, we still like to feel we are masters over our own bodies and that we can flout what nature has given us should we wish to do so. From my client work I have noticed a certain urgency with some GV people to start the physical transition and see change occur as soon as they are able, which I think is reasonable. However, we do need to be mindful that currently there are no requirements for someone who is wishing to access and undertake a medical transition, including hormones and possible intensive surgery, to reflect upon what this might mean for them and being who they sense themselves to be. The Gender GP requires those wishing to access hormones through their services to have some counselling, which I believe is a bold step. Yet, the standard NHS pathway to treatment does not. Of course, the specialist practitioners at the GIC will ask probing questions around the client's gender, but that is not the same as spending regular time reflecting on the experiences the client is facing. There is the 'Real Life Experience', where a client is expected to live full-time in their identified gender for a year (or sometimes two) before the provision of hormones and surgery. However, this in itself is controversial as, while it goes some way to exploring the client's ability to manifest their inner feelings into a meaningful and functioning life, it is far from a perfect, fair and balanced means to determine their ability to take that step into the outside world. I feel that some people starting out on their transition journey are possibly being under-supported and I wonder what the long-term implications of this might be during the years to come.

We will look at the processes that are available to individuals which allow them to manage their physical selves. Firstly, we will look at the types of journeys that GV people typically engage in, as outlined by sociologists Richard Ekins and Dave King in their book *The Transgender Phenomena* (2006). They call this classification 'The modes of gendering and transgendering' and it comprises four parts:

- Gender Migration – most commonly the pathway of the Transsexual as they cross the gender binary (border) from one gender to the other permanently.

- Gender Oscillating – typically expressed as Crossdressing, where individuals cross the gender binary border temporarily.

- Gender Negating – the practice of Sissification is an expression of this behaviour. Where the adult male is forced to crossdress as an ultra-feminine girl, which in that moment negates his masculinity. What is fundamental here is the loss of his hyper-masculinity. This can play the part of sexual fantasies and originates from the BDSM background.

- Gender Transcending – Gender Outlaws and genderqueer are the pathways being travelled here. Their intention is to transcend gender as we know it and refute the gender binary. The 3 entries above here accept the binary in some form, but the outlaw will pick and mix, shift, and reject gender types as they see fit.

(Ekins and King 2006, p.34)

R.I.C.E.S.

Ekins and King say that each of the above subdivisions of GV are the processes by which the individual accomplishes their version of transgendering. The individual will use sub-processes to attain the image that best fits with them. There are five types of phenomena/behaviours (R.I.C.E.S.) which we as therapists need to be mindful of, because when our clients talk of their gendering behaviours these are likely to be what they are referring to:

R – Redefining

I – Implying

C – Concealing

E – Erasing

S – Substituting

Ultimately, the client will be involved in some way in altering their gender signifiers, and usually one of these processes is more dominant than the others.

R.I.C.E.S. are defined as follows:

Redefining – the individual's personal dialogue with and of themselves. The client's own understanding/interpretation of them self, which is based in the phenomena of them gendering their self. However, this cannot occur without the process of them understanding/interpreting and doing their gendered self, and then again understanding/interpreting and doing their gendered self again and again. This is the essence of redefining and is a phenomenon in its own right.

Implying – a process of indicating specific gender signifiers of the intended sex, i.e. wearing 'Breast Forms' or placing something in underpants as a substitute penis 'Packing'.

'Concealing' – a sub process of hiding body parts, e.g. 'Binding Breasts', 'Tucking Penis & Testicles' or wearing a 'Gaff' which is an item which tucks and flattens the penis and testicles. None of these processes are permanent and all can be removed at the end of that specific period of transgendering.

Erasing – eliminating aspects of the physical body which aren't identified with either personally or with the physical sex which the individual identifies with, e.g. growing hair, cutting hair, shaving body hair, wearing a hair piece, wearing/ not wearing makeup etc.

Substituting – dressing style, posture, gesture, speech. The degrees to which the individual undertakes this will depend on varying factors such as age, positions on the continuum, if and how they are 'out', and finances to achieve some of the other aspects within R.I.C.E.S.

(Ekins and King 2006, p.37)

Looking at the list of processes, it's interesting to note that these are used by both cis and GV individuals making adaptations to their bodies via cosmetics, cosmetic surgeries and personal grooming – although the intentions of both groups may be different, the processes are the same.

I have mentioned previously that there are similar patterns or pathways of behaviour that occur throughout the timeline of the GV person's life, in particular transsexual women. There will be personal differences in how they feel and experience themselves, but there are four distinct stages the individual will go through during the development of their gendered self.

The Four Stages of Demystification of the Gender Variant Self-Image

1. The Clothing Phase

This can begin as early as five years of age through to the late twenties. Here the individual becomes aware of, and drawn to, fabrics, textiles, clothing, cosmetics and anything else which would be deemed as not forming part of the birth sex conventions within the particular culture the individual lives in. As an example, I am drawn to texture, colour, form, sheen and how the fabric plays over my body, and how that particular element changes my posture, movement and how I regard myself.

Minor body alterations are explored and employed during the late teens and twenties (e.g. body hair removal, exploring cosmetics, and seeing how clothing and shoes change the body and behaviour). These activities are restricted, or rather regulated, by individual circumstances (i.e. how often the individual is able to find space, time and privacy to be able to do them if they aren't out regarding this aspect of themselves).

Once finances permit, the use of a hair piece, breast forms and body padding or breast binding can allow the connecting together of the internal GI and a now matching external image.

2. The Mirror Moment

This is very similar to a concept which the psychoanalyst Jacques Lacan developed. The concept he called 'The Mirror Stage' was an important early element in his critical reinterpretation of the work of Freud (Evans 2001). Lacan proposes that human infants pass through a stage in which an external image of the body reflected in a mirror produces a psychic response that gives rise to the mental representation of an 'I', a self. The visual identity provided by the mirror supplies imaginary 'wholeness'. Another active factor here is the 'Specular Image':

> Lacan is referring to the reflection of one's own body in the mirror, the image of oneself which is simultaneously oneself and the OTHER (the 'Little' other). It's by identifying with the specular image that the human baby first begins to construct his EGO in the Mirror Stage. (Evans 1996, p.190)

The essence of what Lacan is suggesting is that through the process of 'The Mirror Stage' the child develops their ego via a 'Specular Image', and an aspect of that development is the beginning of a sense of self-identity. The timing of this stage will depend fully on the individual having successfully undertaken and completed the first phase. This is the point where the individual's undertakings of the first phase are now recognised. When all the above components have been assembled, the individual will stand in front of the mirror and see reflected back their own self, which now connects directly to their internal GI. However, there is always that moment where the individual must return to their regular appearance, so it's usual to try to maintain those moments by photographing oneself as a means of preserving a continuance of the image of the identified gendered self beyond the limitations of a hidden activity.

Due to the increase in social media, the next two phases have changed dramatically and do not necessarily occur in the order in which I have listed them below. For many years this was the main way they occurred, but the internet has made reaching out and contacting others a little safer and easier to plan. The flip side to this is that the internet has also corrupted what is an already difficult journey for GV individuals (e.g. sleazy websites where people's attempts to make connections for adult meet-ups, cliques, bitching on forums and misguided advice-giving all take place in an unregulated space). This can be terrifying for first-timers and newbies who are relying on this avenue for safe contact and support.

3. The Public Phase

The individual will make tentative steps to go out into the world, usually very secretly and as safely as they can. This usually takes place under the cover of darkness. It could be to go to the post box at the end of the street, or to go for a drive, ensuring they have a change of clothes in case something untoward occurs. They will not usually make contact with others on these expeditions as the very act of going outside in their presenting gender feels like a huge achievement in itself. On completion of the activity, the sense of achievement is palpable, and addictive. They will usually feel a release from within themselves and isolation from the outside world. This leads to a desire to go out more and take bigger risks, and they now start wanting to meet others like themselves.

4. The Interaction Phase

The individual now actively wishes to seek out others and will take steps to go out as their identified gender with this purpose in mind. They may do this in a number of ways. They may attend an organised group for crossdressers or GV people, run by organisations such as The Beaumont Society or The Northern Concord. Others may meet with friends whom they have met previously online. Some may choose to use the facilities of a dressing service, which for a fee will provide make-up, outfit and hair and then take a group of GV individuals out to a restaurant, nightclub or shopping trip. This is a safe first step for somebody new to going out dressed who doesn't have a safe network of support. Whichever route the individual takes in building a real life out in the world, it produces a heady mix of emotions, and once the individual has tasted it, it becomes really hard to ignore. One client described it to me as: 'Once the genie is out of the bottle, it doesn't want to go back!'

Personal Meaning – Self-Expression Is Not the Same Thing as Self-Identity

Finally, I would like to address the question of self-identity versus self-expression. It feels like in our current version of modern life we are constantly being invited to express ourselves, and not just in relation to GI. With a multitude of technology available, it appears as if it is becoming ever easier should you wish to do so. The problem, as I see it, is, does anyone really have anything meaningful to express? And secondly, I believe that, much in the same way the term 'transgender' has been constantly misused to the point that it has become meaningless, self-expression runs the risk of going the same way. I believe self-identity is a more appropriate term to use in relation to GI than self-expression. So, what is meant by the terms?

Self-expression
Noun
The expression of one's feelings, thoughts, or ideas, especially in writing, art, music, or dance. (Google online dictionary 2018)

That sounds pretty clear and straightforward. It seems here that the essence of this definition is concerned with the expression/communication of one's feelings, thoughts or ideas, from a personal, concentrated, internal position/reaction in relation to something experienced and manifesting a representation of that outside of ourselves in the world. The mediums for manifesting the perception are listed as creative mediums. So, we could interpret self-expression as a reactive behavioural process based on a feeling with an unspecified stimulus.

Now let's look at self-identity:

Self-identity

Noun

The perception or recognition of one's characteristics as a particular individual, especially in relation to social context. (Google online dictionary 2018)

The first thing that comes up for me here is that self-identity is determined by regarding one's personal traits, features, attributes and individuality in relation to some aspect of an external social framework. There is no mention of GI here, and that's okay because the key point of this is that it's about the individual acknowledging some unspecified aspect of what makes them who they are (this could be GI but not exclusively) and undertaking some cognitive and reflective process in regard to themselves and their relationship to the societal structure they live within (maybe how it defines them or not). So, whereas we have a reactive (possibly reflective) behavioural process resulting in an attempt to communicate this to others within a visual format with self-expression, self-identity is certainly more of a personal reflective exploration of aspects of the individual contrasting themselves with their immediate environment and how that defines or conflicts with their personal experience of being in the world.

Thus, we can say that somebody who is articulating their GV as a reflection of their self-identity may use self-expression as the mode by which they choose to convey this. By contrast, if people use self-expression as a means for communicating their feelings, thoughts or ideas, it does not automatically mean that they have engaged in a reflective process which stems from their self-identity – this is what I would recognise as pseudo GV. As I touched on earlier, it is my belief that with the removal of NHS mental health services and the gatekeeping of access to GICs, we have lost a safeguard ensuring that GV clients get a continuous, safe and appropriate care pathway. We are possibly facing the prospect of a situation where some potential GV clients wishing to access a medical transition are exposed to making uninformed choices about appropriate care for their needs; and without the individuals undertaking a rigorous exploration of their experience in relation to GI, we may see more cases of pseudo GV.

I make no apologies for keeping the language used as simple and as day-to-day as possible because I regard the use of language and its personal meaning as the reason why a lot of words lose their specific meaning – as we have seen with objective and subjective reality, the same can occur when words end up adrift and far from what we consider they might actually mean. This has been the fate of the word 'transgender', and although there will be some readers who will think I'm pedantic for refusing to use it within the context of this book and replacing it with 'gender variance', it is my hope that if practitioners can begin to apply 'gender variance' for a time, we might be able to decontaminate the word 'transgender' with a view to re-using it more appropriately. We have seen by our little exploration of self-expression and self-identity that these two terms are again not the same thing, even though they now seem to be heading towards the same fate as 'transgender'. In my mind, the appropriate and careful use of language when working with and talking about GV is fundamental in ensuring clarity of meaning.

EXERCISE 5: PERSONAL MEANING – PART 3

While the theory is fresh in your mind, please answer the following questions:

What kind of woman are you?

Or

What kind of man are you?

If you're struggling with these, try to apply the Phenomenological Method as its rules can lead you to a clearer, more open response.

Once you have answered one, maybe you could try the other!

Make some notes and keep them to hand for Chapter 9.

CHAPTER 8

THE PHENOMENOLOGY
OF TRANSITION

There are many false understandings around the experience of what happens when a person begins the actual process of a medical transition or living full-time. There is an unhealthy interest in some aspects of the process, and certainly the media overly focuses on the surgery, whereas in my mind the physical aspect of transition is a small proportion of the actual journey.

I intend this chapter to provide the reader with a flavour of what life was like for me when dealing with certain aspects of the medical transition and crossing the gender border and beginning to live full-time. It would be incorrect to suggest that what I experienced was/is typical for all GV people. However, what I can confirm from my client work is that the themes I raise within this chapter are consistent to varying degrees amongst people walking similar paths to myself. I am keen to present the phenomena/ occurrences of what life can be like once we get behind the hyperbole of how the media present the GV experience. The reality is that this journey isn't glamorous/exotic or special in any way, unlike how the social and conventional media sources have chosen to present it. Yes, it can be hard-going (but whose life isn't?), but it is, for the most part, normal, dull and commonplace (which is exactly how I like it). However, I'd be doing it a disservice if I didn't mention the highlights (who would put themselves through this unless the price was worth paying?), and lowlights too. Most of all, I feel that all this media interest has contributed to an us-and-them culture, with GV people being presented as very different to cissexual people. This, I believe, is quite unhealthy and can lead to the continuation of GV people not being taken seriously, with the worst-case outcomes being transphobia and GV hate crime.

The other theme I want to draw your attention to in this chapter is that although the pathway for a GV individual reaching their actualised self may not be easy or something that cissexual people may identify with, the day-to-day hopes and fears of both GV and cissexual people are ultimately the same – we are all human.

> **Wednesday 23 April 2014:** After what had felt like forever the day has arrived where I begin the medical transition and start taking oestrogen. I am starting off on 2 mg of Progynova. This feels like a tiny dose to my untrained mind and I wonder how such a small increment of hormone will be able to afford any noticeable process of change within my body. In that moment I am reminded of what the specialist at Charing Cross GID clinic said when he agreed to begin the prescribing process. 'We'll start you on a low dose to begin with to make sure it doesn't kill you!'

I could have been mistaken in believing that this was merely banter; however, seeing as he hadn't made any attempts at humour in the previous 45 minutes of the session, I uncomfortably accepted that he was being quite serious. Suddenly those 2 mg felt inordinately powerful, and once they were inside my body that was it… I was along for the ride. I felt it strange that despite the years of misusing alcohol to achieve a mental condition which made my experience of being in the world a little less painful,

I had never remotely been interested in taking recreational drugs – in fact, they scared me witless. It was the same feeling I experienced within this moment as I took those two tiny tablets. As I washed them down with a glass of water and they were inside me, I felt trepidation that now I was along for the ride and there was no getting off! This was it. This was the first physical step in connecting the inside and outside of myself.

Within 45 minutes to 1 hour I experienced the very first effects of the oestrogen while I was driving to work – and, no, it wasn't sudden breast or hair growth. To begin with it felt like a gradual warm platinum-coloured trickle within my brain. It felt good, it felt very good. I imagined it to be what a recreational drug-user might seek out when they took their drug of choice. Within the next 30 minutes the trickle became a beautiful shiny platinum-coloured surge coursing throughout the whole of my body. To say it felt good doesn't do the feeling justice. It was the best I had ever felt in my entire life. Looking at my notebook of what I wrote on that day as I attempted to capture and convey the feeling, the description I used was: 'Euphoric and bullet proof.' I felt awesome and wondered if this was how other people felt about themselves. I parked my car at work, grabbed my bag and strode in with a sense of power, strength and surety in myself – that was a very new experience. As I went into the building I thought to myself: *'Madison has arrived!'*

Thursday 29 May 2014: Had a blood test to check that all was fine and that it was going to be okay to be able to commence the planned increase of oestrogen up to the full daily dose of 4 mg. In the weeks following beginning HRT, initial euphoria and bullet proof feeling has continued, and I feel I am managing my life so much better than I have ever done so before. This is an unexpected and welcome change. There is some understanding on online forums of the potential psychological changes that have occurred. A blanket of calmness is what is usually reported in terms of psychological effects. Becoming overly emotional is also what I have heard reported, so I feel myself to be incredibly fortunate and blessed with what I have had occur. In terms of physical changes, nothing much to report other than a slight softening of the skin on my elbows of all places!

Thursday 5 June 2014: Discovered that the results from the blood test have been lost, so I return to have a second lot of bloods taken. Frustration at this incompetence; yet another hold-up! It's times like this when I feel personal progress is outside my control.

Thursday 12 June 2014: Receive a phone call from my GP that the bloods are all fine and he is happy to increase the prescription to 4 mg. It would appear the HRT isn't killing me!

A possible point to note is that when hormones are prescribed the actual tablets are the exact same tablets which are prescribed to biological women when they begin a course of HRT following the onset of the menopause. As such, the packaging and information leaflet are solely aimed for this prescribing group. This means there is no specific information for GV women on the safe taking of the hormones and their possible side effects. Yes, the GIC provides a small amount of information on the physical effects of taking the oestrogen, but there is no information provided about any of the psychological and emotional effects. This, I believe, is a poor duty of care, as I can confirm that I and most of the GV clients I have worked with have experienced some moderate negative changes to their moods or psychological well-being.

Tuesday 29 July 2014: Since the last update, I have experienced the very beginnings of some physical breast development. The two main changes are a slight increase in size and itching, lots of itching (this wasn't included in the info sheet, but it's obvious that this is part of the growth process). I have been told by two separate people that my physical shape has changed already. I cannot see it myself, but it's always curious when I get separate and unconnected observations, which on enquiry were saying similar things – mainly that I'm beginning to curve and soften. My skin is more generally softening now, and this is a nice unexpected change (and, no, this wasn't included in the info sheet from the GIC).

Psychologically, things were not so positive. The euphoria and bullet-proofness had given way to low and unstable moods. I was beginning each day by sitting at the end of the bed with tearful and suicidal feelings of 'What's the point in living?!' Now, if it hadn't been for my professional background, this would have done for me. But researching the psychological side effects and knowing that my life was in pretty good shape clarified that what I was experiencing was due to the HRT. Once I got past these feelings first thing each morning, the rest of the days were a mixture of feeling depressed and unable to cope with my day or feelings, a sense of worthlessness, and a most pronounced paranoia. Some of my male-to-female transsexual clients have experienced very similar low and changeable moods. Quite a large number find that the commencement of hormones is a huge step and they were quite unprepared when the low moods kicked in and disrupted their daily function. I remember one female-to-male transsexual client who developed considerable aggression at the start of HRT. I remember them attending a session feeling deeply distressed and tearful as the previous evening they had experienced an outburst of aggression like they had never experienced before in their life. This anger had nearly culminated in physical aggression towards their long-term partner. They hadn't expected this. Once we had discussed the situation, it was understandable what had happened. Just knowing made them feel less at the mercy of the emotions triggered by the hormones. A simple bit of education by the GIC could have prevented this distress to both my client and their partner.

Monday 4 August 2014: The breast itching has been joined by pain in them also.

Sunday 10 August 2014: I have noticed a slight lifting of the low moods. This is a blessing as it's all been rather exhausting.

Tuesday 12 August 2014: I have begun voice coaching to address the fact that even though my appearance is very clearly female, when I open my mouth I certainly do not sound female. I have been wondering though why I am doing this coaching. What I have felt is that the voice I have seen beginning to emerge during the sessions doesn't feel like me. It doesn't feel like I want to inhabit that voice and it doesn't fit the way I am. So, I'm questioning whether I am doing the coaching for others around me so that I look and feel more consistent and there's less of a discord between my look and my sound. This transition is mine and not anyone else's.

Yes, I get misgendered on the phone most of the time and it really irritates me and I get quite fed up with having to explain myself and then feeling bad when the person on the other end gets worried that they have upset me. I then find myself having to apologise for them getting upset because I wanted to clarify this with them. The misgendering is going to happen. I'm a realist, but it frustrates the hell out of me when it's happening with my bank when I've given them all the paperwork of my transition and they have put a note on my file. In these cases, the confusion is purely because the person on the other end of the phone has not bothered to read the note on my file, the very note that is there to prevent such occurrences. Sometimes things feel more complicated than they need to be.

In the end I decided that the voice that was evolving wasn't right for me and I didn't wish to pursue voice coaching. As I spend most of my days talking as a therapist – that's what I do – I was also told that I wouldn't be able to affect the voice all the time as I could damage my vocal chords. So in the end, if

I was going to be limited as to how long I could use a voice I wasn't happy with, then it seemed a moot point and I decided to invest my energies in other things. I still get fed up with the misgendering, but I think I have learnt to not let it distress me like it once did. I have learnt to pick my battles and to choose wisely where I invest my energy.

Sunday 17 August 2014: My moods have been up and down recently, but I would say there's been nothing unbearable. I don't feel there has been as much physical development as I would have wished/hoped there to be. I don't know if this is just my perception or the reality. Maybe I'm impatient?

Sunday 14 September 2014: My moods have really levelled out now, or at least they don't feel as savage as they once were. Still finding my emotional life tough under the circumstances, but the type of emotional distress now feels proportionate to what is actually occurring within my life rather than having suicidal thoughts with no real reason for them (i.e. I knew that life was alright and certainly didn't warrant the extremes of emotions). The main reason now for my emotional unhappiness is that I have become estranged from my family due to me coming out to them about my GI earlier this year. Hardest thing is there is no open dialogue about this, which for me as a therapist feels incredibly difficult and backward. I will keep trying to communicate the positives of my transition, as they wanted me to be happy and I am.

I have been experiencing pains in my left testicle. They are sharp and come and go with no obvious trigger. I cannot find any explicit reason for this other than thinking it might be something related to the HRT. In five weeks I am due to return to Charing Cross GIC. I am feeling very unsettled and feel restless to augment the oestrogen with some anti-androgens which would really clamp down on my testosterone production and give the oestrogen space to develop and change my body. I'm going through a period of hatred for my body.

Roughly six months have elapsed since I commenced HRT and I am uncomfortable with my male form. It feels like the female physical form is beneath this male shell and that she is now trying to break through the surface. I'm itching and hurting, and I'm so done with a physical form which I have struggled to inhabit and make work for my life so far.

Monday 6 October 2014: Since my last update the main points of note are that my breasts continue to be uncomfortable. The breast pain is at its most painful come late afternoon and early evening; and if knocked, the pain is excruciating. To try and remedy this, I have taken to sleeping wearing a padded sports bra to ease the discomfort.

This is something I continued to do for the next year or so whilst the breasts reached their full development within a 2–3-year timescale following the commencement of taking oestrogen. An interesting point to note is that the optimum size of the neo-breast based on HRT alone is one cup size smaller than that of the individual's mother.

As for the testicular pain, after consulting my GP and being advised to monitor the discomfort, the pain stopped as suddenly as it had started.

Saturday 19 September 2015: A bit of a gap since my last update as things have ticked along pretty much as they had been. Today I will focus on how things have evolved since I wrote here last: the changes that have occurred, with the unexpected, and in some cases disappointing, developments due to these occurrences.

It feels strange to me (even though I know maybe it shouldn't surprise me, knowing the human species as I have come to over the years of being involved in my profession, and more generally having an interest in human behaviour) that there is an over-fascination in GV people's bodies and the phenomena around effemimania (the presentation of male femaling in its many forms). At the time of this diary entry, the tsunami of public frenzy around GV had not quite made landfall, but even so there was an unhealthy interest in the physical part of the transition process by the cis public.

Having now been on my physical journey over the gender border I have had time to reflect and recognise that the physical transition is perhaps around only 30–40 per cent maximum of the overall process. It's been said before, but I will say it again: We are so much more than what is between our legs.

What makes this part of the book a phenomenological enquiry rather than a journal, diary or biography is that I want to explore the 'being' of GI as a phenomenon, and how it's experienced rather than what happened. To this end I have decided to be brutally open about what it means for me to have travelled over the gender border full-time. I think that the media has become fully absorbed in focusing on the physical aspects of GV rather than covering everything else that is occurring. As I have shown at various times throughout this book, the process of my own GI's evolution had been present for most of my life. It was within my capability to understand what I was experiencing in relation to myself and my peers and then to make sense of what it was. This was going to be partly governed by society's own understanding in relation to gender but also by how my own specific living environment permitted my exploration of my GI. This is pretty much the same narrative for many GV people. However, this latent physical stage of GV, as I shall refer to it, is not always understood or articulated as clearly as other stages later in the individual's life. This can create a certain mystification, which I think is sometimes reinforced by GV people (or, at the very least down-played), that when they begin living in their authentic gender (or as it is more commonly referred to, 'going/living full-time') that on a specific day they now present as the GI they feel is a true reflection of themselves. I am specifically referring here to transsexuals. Gender fluid, queer and non-binary people are also likely to have a time where they commit to living their version of authenticity, yet I believe for transsexual people, their transition is by its very nature a more public and multi-dimensional overt realignment, for when the male to female steps across the gender border, they also relinquish male privileges (e.g. social power). This therefore places some greater expectations on the individual to present from day one of their transition as a reasonable-to-perfect presentation of femaleness. We must remind ourselves of the social pressures that exist for biological women to present themselves in the most perfect versions of femininity, so how does someone who was born a biological male yet experiences a version of the GV phenomena meet such expectations of physical/social presentation? The thing is, day one of living full-time rarely begins with the GV individual being altogether prepared and naturally presenting. It will be a sliding scale for everyone of how much progress has been achieved and in what areas before commencing full-time.

You see, despite me making every effort to present a coherent day-to-day presentation publicly (which reduces the feelings of gender dysphoria), I didn't expect to find that this wouldn't be the case in my private world, where I regularly find that I and my presentation drift. Until this point only a handful of people knew that my public daily presentation isn't as fixed as most people might imagine. I am thankful that I have learnt a successful proficiency of 'Implying' and 'Substituting' the aspects of myself which need some assistance in achieving the impression I wish to consistently present to the public. However, this image relies on these processes to achieve something close to my actualised self, reducing my dysphoria, and permitting me to achieve the 'Mirror Moment' where the circle becomes complete and the inner and outer worlds connect for the first time.

There is a public misconception that on the day the individual transitions and begins living 'full-time' they are beginning that life complete, and this completeness is absolute. The reality is very different, and I think that the language used (i.e. 'full-time') is where this mistaken belief comes from. Evidence to support this is that even after all this time and emotional investment I am realistically 'self-actualised' for only some of the time (I am aware that this is also the case for a lot of other transsexual women). There are days when preparing to go out in public feels more like a makeover than a confirmation of GI, yet there is so much more to living full-time in the gender role that I sense myself to be, and that is the invisible stuff. For me as a transsexual woman writing at this point in my border crossing, there are the complex factors of social position/relationships, and being interpreted as I am presenting by those around me (I don't carry a sign saying 'Hi, please note that I am trying to look like a woman, so if you can please regard me as such I should be extremely grateful, thanks'). These social and presentation aspects are of equal importance to the physical changes, and yet there are never any discussions or preparations for these huge factors and how the GV individual will deal with them. It's quite easy to see how some GV people get so easily upset when they present as their authentic self and society doesn't instantly accept or understand them. Although slightly different, it reminds me of the fairy tale 'The Emperor's New Clothes', by Hans Christian Andersen, about an emperor who pays a lot of money for some new magic clothes which can only be seen by wise people. The clothes do not really exist, but the emperor does not admit he cannot see them, because he does not want to seem stupid. Now I am certainly not saying that GV individuals are delusional – far from it – but when they/ we/I go out in public, there are certain unspoken phenomena that hopefully will take place between the GV person and the cis members of society that they encounter. And that is that they are regarded in the way that society regards people of that specific sex. A casual slip of the tongue can be enough to damage a fragile SC.

After 18 months on hormones and living publicly full-time, I find myself still being forced to dip in and out and I have times when I'm forced to see my old self. I've come to label my full-time self as my 'constructed surface self', and this feels cruel because when I present as that self all feels fine, but I still see remnants of my old self, which feels like a bit of a come-down. I am still wearing breast forms and I am now going to be dependent on wearing a hairpiece for the rest of my life. I, like a lot of male-to-female GV women, have natural hair which is unaffected by the introduction of oestrogen. I wasn't made aware there was a possibility of this when I was discussing commencing hormones with the GIC back in 2013. It was a real disappointment and one I think will take me some time to begin to accept.

Saturday 26 September 2015: I had my first test-patch of electrolysis hair removal today. A one-and-a-half-inch square was worked on, which took 10 minutes to complete. It felt like I had been mugged by a swarm of bees – sting after sting rained down on my cheek, just below my right ear. The pain was already unpleasant enough and left me feeling sore. Then the technician said I would probably require 1,500 hours of electrolysis to get me to where I wanted to be. And at £30 per one-hour session [I'll let you do the maths] I felt like I'd been slapped firmly in the face!

The NHS will cover the cost of 20 sessions of facial hair removal and whatever genital hair removal is required to get me surgery-ready, even though all that sounds harsh, I think that I am going to struggle to undertake that much discomfort over such a long time. I think I'm going to need to reconsider my hair-removal options.

Wednesday 4 November 2015 – Monday 23 November 2015: My mother took my decision to transition quite hard. Both she and my father withdrew for a few months to try and make sense of the changes. They chose not to speak to me and, whilst not liking this, I respected their wishes and kept contact to a minimum. I offered practical support in the form of information for families and friends of the GV loved one. I was hoping that this would show them that what was happening, although hard for them, wasn't something completely unheard of. I started receiving letters from my mother stating that they were so hurt by my decision to transition and wishing I had said something before. In fact, I had tested the water a few years earlier and, knowing how averse my parents were to anything outside their comfort zone, I presented my disclosure of crossdressing in a very low-key fashion. I was quite surprised by their response – my mother said, 'You're our child and we want you to be happy.' This felt like a huge step had been made, but circumstances and a lack of life security meant there would be no further developments in this area for five years. Such time had passed that I began to wonder if I had ever had that conversation with my parents and maybe I had imagined the whole thing.

By the time I practically outed myself with my mother during the phone call where she wanted me to only wear my normal clothes on my next visit to see them, it was clear to me that I had to disclose to my parents I was transitioning and that I would be living full-time. What did start to burn away for me once the letters started trickling through was that things didn't appear to be getting easier. I had been told that they had decided that they weren't going to tell family and friends that I had transitioned and that they couldn't accept me as anyone other than Mark, their son. I felt very saddened to learn I had become a shameful secret. What had happened to me being their child and they wanting me to be happy? I felt cheated of this happiness that appeared to be conditional.

Over the next few years Mum started to regain some strength and eventually agreed to meet me. The first visit she was very tearful, but she and I got through the two hours at a very quiet garden centre outside the small town of Tadley. I felt pleased to have met with her and to have answered her questions and to begin getting to know one another again as I felt their estrangement from me had changed us all.

I started to see my mum again. She even said she would do what she could to try and see if she could unstick my father's intransigent position. This would be one of three meet-ups I had with her over the next few years. The next was at a Newbury motorway service area, where we sat on an outside bench in the coach park with hordes of tourists milling about one August bank holiday. The final meeting was at Tina's and my home in Peterborough the following summer. My mum was unwell but in good spirits. At each visit, my mum, who wasn't a fan of driving, had been transported by my father, and each time he didn't want any contact with me. I saw him from a distance at the motorway services when Tina went over to say hello, and outside in the car when he brought Mum to our home. We were all getting older, everything was changing and life was slipping by. I felt incredibly frustrated that his stubbornness was keeping the family fragmented. One day it would be too late and there would be no more chances to repair the damage. And one day, the clock did finally run out of time for us.

Tina took the short phone call from my father and came through to where I was sitting in my office. I could see her preparing to buffer me from the information that she had been asked to pass on to me (I kind of was expecting it). 'That was your dad, Mads. He's asked me to let you know that your mum passed away yesterday.' That was it. Regardless of how difficult things had been, my hope that one day we would be a family again was gone. A child-like fantasy it may have been, but for me there had been a small amount of hope that everything would be okay and that the hard times and the rejection were not for nothing. I was struck by a sudden confusion which overtook me. I felt I wanted to be upset but found it quite hard to do so. I had been living with such a distance from my parents over the last few years that I think I had come to put our relationships on the outside because I had found that to keep trying to make things right was so very exhausting. It was a confused place that I wouldn't resolve for some time. The next emotion I experienced hit me unexpectedly and I was fully unprepared:

'Mum died yesterday?' I said to Tina, and she nodded.

'Apparently your brother was there with him when she passed,' Tina added.

'So, it's taken him 24 hours to tell me,' I said. 'He must have known in plenty of time she was going to pass away if he managed to communicate with my brother, who then had to arrange to fly down from Scotland to Hampshire! Yet he didn't ring me to give me the time to make the 2-hour drive!'

Rage... I was filled with rage, so now not only did I have to come to terms with the loss, but my lasting memory of Mum dying was being furious with my father for what was callous and as I felt at the time unforgivable; however, it was going to get worse.

Over the next few days my father and I spoke on the phone for the first time in four years. I felt that maybe something was changing in our relationship for the better. But there was something unspoken between us. It was so obvious by its absence as it pressed heavily in the silences of our communications. Not once did he mention my mother's funeral. Tina and I did a quick bit of research online and discovered when and where it was taking place. So, by the time we were a few days away from the day of the funeral and he still hadn't mentioned anything regarding it, I decided it was time to do something I'd been terrified of doing all my life with this man: it was time to challenge him.

'So, how are the funeral arrangements going?' I enquired.

'Yes, everything has been sorted,' he replied.

'Okay. Well that's pretty good going as it's the day after tomorrow. When were you going to tell me the dates and times of it?'

My speech was starting to break with a combination of the anger and anxiety I was feeling.

The silence was palpable. My father finally broke the silence.

'Well, I don't want you there, so I didn't feel we needed to go into details.'

Inside I felt my rage surging to the surface and boiling out of me, although my speech was decidedly calm.

'Okay, let me just confirm what I think you have just said. So not only have you prevented me from seeing my mother before she passed, you're now telling me that you don't want me at her funeral. That's correct, yes?'

'She didn't want to see you.'

'Well I'm sorry, the crematorium is a public space and if I want to pay my respects to my mother's memory then that's what I will do, right!'

It took all my strength to not send a tirade of abuse in his direction.

'Yes, the crematorium is a public place, but if you attend I will not acknowledge you and I will never have anything else to do with you.'

I decided to cease the communication at that point as I was ready to say things which wouldn't help the situation. I was hollowed out and numb by what I had just heard. I felt like I was being erased from what remained of my family. Ultimately, I decided I couldn't put myself through the stress of the journey and any hostility I might encounter. My father said he would ignore me, but my brother has a temper on him and I really didn't want a scene. Mum deserved better than that. So, I and a few friends and some of Tina's family held a very small and impromptu service of memorial for Mum on the day of her funeral. It wasn't ideal, but it was the best that we could do under the circumstances. I have come to know that there is much to be said about grieving within the group of people who knew the deceased. Solitary grief has felt like howling into the void.

Saturday 28 November 2015: My father kindly sent an order of service from my mum's funeral. It arrived in the post today. Sadness turns to rage as I read the acknowledgements at the back of the booklet: 'Paul and Lee would wish to thank you for your heartfelt messages of support and kind words of comfort after the sad loss of a much-loved wife, mum, grandma and friend.'

My father had chosen to not include me or mention me in any way. She was my mum, and he erased me from the family at such a significant time. I was completely removed from this event and that is how it will always be. What also continues to upset me is that he lied to all who attended to account for my absence. Family and friends will now be left with the belief that I chose to stay away from my own mother's funeral. Yes, I did, but not because I wanted to. And all this because my father and brother see me as something shameful.

Thursday 14 January 2016: I'm taking the short walk from the office car park to my desk, a walk of no more than six minutes. I've just crossed the road where I was transphobically shouted at by a pack of workmen last year (all that CCTV and not one camera was working!) and I am at the steps outside my office building. As I negotiate my bags and office security swipe card, I become aware of someone behind me. I think nothing of it as the building is usually quite busy and I fumble to swipe my card to gain entrance and to pull the big red door whilst holding my baggage and trying to keep an air of composure. As I turn and go through the door and momentarily hold the door, I see that behind me is a short man in his mid- to late twenties, with a stubbled face and dressed in smart casual. As I hold the door for him to follow behind me, I smile, but it's a smile of politeness and I don't give anything emotional away with it, other than being polite.

I begin ascending the first flight of stairs and he follows a step or two behind me. I feel uncomfortable as he isn't a familiar face in the building. After three years working there, I've got to know a face even if I don't know them personally. As I round the first flight of stairs, on the second, the stairs naturally turn me to face him and I see him smiling at me.

'Hello, you're very pretty!' he says with an accent.

'Oh no!' I say to myself, as a huge chasm of fear opens within me and my personal protection is suddenly thrown into question.

Okay, so let me point out a few things here about what this situation highlights regarding GV women getting hit on by men. Firstly, we need to clarify that each situation is defined by the individuals present and their possible intentions. If we look at the kind of language used in this topic, it should clarify some of the prejudices at play. You see, there are a variety of terms, inside both the transgender and academic communities, for people who are attracted to transgender people. These terms include 'admirer', 'transfan', 'trans catcher', 'trans erotic', 'transsensual', 'transoriented', 'tranny chaser' and 'tranny hawk', though the final two may be considered offensive as they contain a slur. The term 'tranny chaser' was originally (and is still predominantly) used to describe men sexually interested in visibly trans women, but it is now used by some trans men as well. Transgender people often use the term in a pejorative sense, because they consider chasers to value them for their trans status alone, rather than being attracted to them as a person. However, some claim this term in an affirming manner. The term 'tranny' (or 'trannie') is itself considered a slur in many circles.

According to Jeffrey Escoffier of the Center for Gay and Lesbian Studies at CUNY, sexual interest in trans women first emerged in 1953, associated with the public interest in Christine Jorgensen (Escoffier 2011). It was after SRS became more feasible during the 1960s that sexual orientation came to be re-conceptualised as distinct from GI and crossdressing. In a survey of men who engage in sex with trans women, 73–92 per cent identified their sexual identity as straight or bisexual (Escoffier 2011).

Now I cannot and would not profess to make a generalisation regarding what motivates these kinds of guys to be attracted to GV females, because it would be personal for every individual. However, I can tell you what I've learned over the years: some are interested in the whole 'chick with a dick' fantasy. Others would class themselves as heterosexual but are curious because the GV fem offers some kind of exotic distraction. There are some whose cultural background has an acceptance that GV women are no different to biological women. Other guys are genuinely attracted to GV girls because they have no concerns about the girl's history and they are first and foremost a person attracted to another person; they see the relationship as straight; end of.

However, there are some men who regard themselves to be straight, yet find themselves in a social situation where they are attracted to a woman and they approach to engage in adult conversation with possible adult outcomes. They may discover the woman to be GV and they see this as possibly a deception. They may then react violently. There are also cases where men interpret this attraction as a failing in their heterosexuality and they lash out because the thought that they are not 100 per cent hetero is unthinkable to them.

If we return to my predicament, firstly, without wanting to big up my ego, this was not the first time I had experienced a guy approaching or presenting interest in me whilst out in public presenting as female. The first time it happened was when I was living in Hackney Wick in East London and I was walking up the long slope to enter the overland railway station. There was only myself and a guy there as it was a quiet time of day. As I was walking up the ramp into the station he wolf-whistled at me and shouted out that he thought I was of interest to him. I experienced a very brief feeling of 'Okay, this is pretty cool' as he found me attractive and therefore I must be presenting well. This was short-lived and was suddenly washed aside with the thought: 'What if he hasn't realised I'm a variation of female? If he discovers this, then I'm possibly going to be in trouble.' I increased my pace up the ramp and I noticed the train I wanted was coming into the station. I walked as far down the platform as I could, to get to a carriage that he wouldn't be able to access. Thankfully, on this occasion things worked out and by the time I got to Kings Cross station I was able to get off the train and disappear into the mass of commuters. Now I don't want to assume that all men are like this, and this chap may have been totally harmless and in no way a threat, but in the moment of being alone on a quiet street and a possibly deserted railway platform, I had to make a call on keeping myself safe.

The second experience occurred when I had moved up to Peterborough and lived with Tina. I wasn't presenting full-time but I did like to go out en femme when I was able. So, on one occasion on a quiet Saturday morning when I was thoroughly absorbed in browsing through the clothing department in one of the local department stores, I became aware that there was somebody just out of eyesight. As I moved so did they, and without looking up I continued with my browsing. I rounded a clothing display carousel and finally stood opposite my shadow. I looked up to see who had been just out of eyesight and was met with a beaming smile from a young Asian guy. I nervously smiled a reply and then turned to the net clothing rail. However, now he had made eye contact he was going to be more forthright in his pursuit. He moved with me and stood right next to me while I avoided eye contact. Without prompting he spoke up and said, 'Hello, you're a very pretty lady!'

I was in two minds as to whether I should reply but I'm not a rude person, and although this was mildly annoying I didn't feel threatened as I had done in my first experience a year or two earlier. So, I replied with a 'Thank you' and moved onto the next rack of clothing. As before, he came with me. Perhaps my polite reply had been received as encouragement, as he suddenly made his intentions quite clear to me: 'You pretty lady and you give me your phone number and we can meet up for fun, yes!'

The way he said this sounded less of a question and rather more that we *would* be having fun. Well, that was it. I was well over caring about being polite and I turned to him and said: 'Excuse me, but I'd prefer if you would leave me alone, please. I'm not going to be giving you my phone number and may I suggest you keep this kind of behaviour for nightclubs, not department stores!'

With that, I turned and walked off, feeling rather empowered by my reaction. I think I was able to do this because I felt safe in the environment. This is not how I was feeling when the first incident occurred.

Thursday 14 January 2016: I am alone, and my mind is full of lots of different questions which I'd prefer answers to before I respond. But alas, as with my previous experiences, I don't have the luxury of knowing who and what kind of situation I am dealing with. Does he know who I am? Is that what his interest is? Or does he see me as biologically female? And if he doesn't know, how will he react if he finds out? I'm now less than 12 metres from my office door but it might as well be 24 metres because of the panic that's rising up within me. Without making eye contact I reply with a 'Thank you'.

I have reached the top step and turn to the office's main door. I push worries about whether my voice has given away who I am and grab my swipe card again. As I do so, a voice behind me speaks up: 'Can I have your phone number?' I determinedly swipe my card and heave the heavy door and partially step through and turn to the direction of the voice behind me and firmly say 'No', whilst letting the door slam shut with an echoing clunk behind me.

I am safe. But what I'm not safe from are all the thoughts running through my head. I'm left with many uninvited questions which have unloaded themselves upon me: Had I passed (been a biological female)? Perhaps he knew who I was, which would mean he might be an admirer, and this would mean my attempts to present as realistically female are transparent and I'm obviously kidding myself that I am able to live convincingly female.

My head is full of confusion, frustration and anger and I momentarily want to find him and ask him what it was that he was attracted to. That madness passes but the doubt sits heavily within me for some time.

CHAPTER 9

DEBUNKING GENDER

Dare We Be Ourselves? And Towards a Gender-Positive Therapy

So, it's no wonder most people assume that I must be mentally ill, because in this culture, wanting to be a woman is something most people find literally unimaginable. And when I do have my SRS, my surgical deconstructed genitals will no doubt be seen by some to be an abomination or a blasphemy. Because my cunt will be the ultimate question mark, asking, how powerful can the penis really be if the sane and smart person like me decide she can do without it? And if the world supposedly revolves around the penis then, my SRS will knock it off its axis. And phallic symbols everywhere will come crashing down like nothing more than a House of Cards. After all, a cigar is always just a cigar. And I am simply me. And I'm fed up with other people projecting their penis obsessions onto my body. As far as I'm concerned, if they can't fathom why I might want to trade in my penis for a clitoris and vagina, then they're the ones who have the gender disorder.

(Serano 2006, p.231)

As we have seen throughout this book, there is much confusion around the language used in identifying and communicating GI, and this is one of the main reasons why society struggles to fully grasp gender's subtle and nuanced nature. Add to this the personal subjectivity of meaning and it's a recipe for confusion. A quick glance at any social media or gender-related thread will show you the emotionally charged chaos that can ensue when the gender deniers tout their limited repertoire: 'Men have penises, women have breasts and vaginas. So, if you have a penis, you're a man; and if you don't, you're a woman. End of!' To them it is simply black and white, and nice and binary, and anyone who says that it's otherwise is either crazy or making things up. The other problem we face is belief in a gender binary truth, and anyone challenging that view is thought to stand on shaky ground. As the French post-Freudian psychoanalyst Jacques Lacan postulated, 'society has come to view gender as a universal truth which we accept without question' (Evans 1996).

These two factors – a 'binary truth' and language confusion – are a potent mixture that ensures that the evolution and our understanding of GI are going to be turbulent. The language used is clumsy and prejudiced, and often results in us stumbling around grasping for something palpable; yet at the same time we're not certain about what exactly it is we are trying to determine about ourselves. An example of this crass understanding at work is the now tired and outdated phrase 'I am a woman trapped inside a man's body!' What does that even mean?!

Think about it... There is a sense of the individual saying that it's their belief they know what it feels like to be a woman. Perhaps they are saying that they are like GV Russian dolls. There is a lot being assumed and guessed, and I feel that this phrase is empty speech made up of poorly selected, lazily chosen and assembled words. The 'woman trapped' quote shows us it can be hard to define and communicate accurately what our experience of our gender is for us. The complexity in defining it, coupled with us living in a world where we are expected to live according to the binary model, can lead us to feel as if the very essence of GI eludes our senses, with it only being perceptible in fleeting, ephemeral glimpses. I described it in the Introduction as something 'uncanny'. It inhabits us with a delicate vigour, and only the passing of time allows it to communicate its presence. However, unravelling and making sense of it can cause us mental anguish, as we fathom our way through our CoW which have piled in on top of this essence over the years, resulting in a significant piece of psychological archaeology as we try to uncover and interpret these feelings. Meanwhile, society continuously puts out messages of conformity and belonging and being part of an acceptable norm. With these pressures upon us we can run the risk of misconstruing what it is we are picking up about ourselves and understanding this. Therefore, I believe we will see a rise in the coming years of people requesting to detransition, because they misinterpreted the signals and wrongly believed that transitioning would make their life a whole lot easier.

I see it is as our duty as clinical practitioners to assist our GV clients in determining a language that is in touch with their gender essence, and with the use of techniques such as those covered within this book to enable the client to find a language that speaks clearly and meaningfully of their experience of GI.

The Trouble with Gender Variance

So, what of these gender outlaws...the gender variants, the transgendered, the non-binary and those ploughing their own furrow within society? The reality is I'm talking about us all! We are all GV, having not really ever been 100 per cent male or female at either end of the continuum. We're all ploughing our own furrows, and it isn't my place to tell you that your assignment as male or female when you entered this world was wrong or that whoever pronounced 'Congratulations, it's a boy/girl' at your birth was way off the mark. Yet as we have observed throughout this book, those of us who are hegemonic males or emphasised females are really few and far between.

Paradoxically, in society at this moment in time, the problem we have is made worse to a degree by having a gender split between cissexuals and GV folk. I've called this section 'The Trouble with Gender Variance', which isn't completely fair as I could have easily have called it 'The Trouble with Cissexuals'. Either way, the problem when presented as an 'either/or' is that it creates an 'us and them' situation. This situation, with its dualistic component, can – as history has shown over thousands of years and in many different instances (i.e. culture, religion, sex and GI) – lead to right and wrong, winners and losers, good and evil. Who is more valid than who?

We as a species aren't always very tolerant when it comes to differences between one group of people and another. As we saw in Chapter 2, the conquistadors dehumanised the New World peoples, and once the latter were considered 'an-other' it was very easy for the former to begin treating them with contempt. Even today, when difference is not fully understood or even feared by the commonly recognised majority, it can be seen as a threat; and we know only too well how as a species we deal with threats and how some individuals deal with perceived threats by using extreme measures. Figure 2, 'The Pyramid of Hate', illustrates the various stages of how difference is treated.

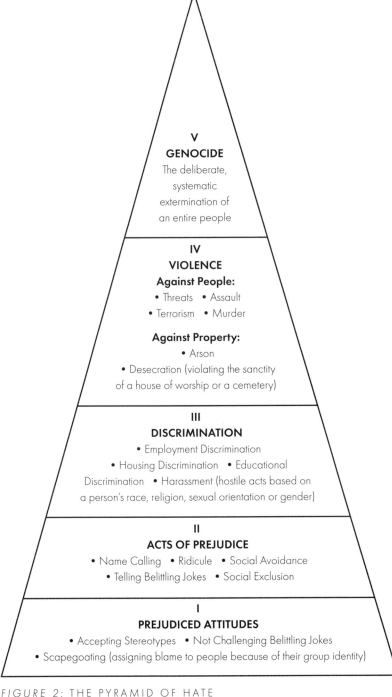

FIGURE 2: THE PYRAMID OF HATE

(Anti-Defamation League 2003)

Thankfully, the explosion of attention around GI over the last few years hasn't all been negative, and it certainly has led to improvements in the quality of life for many GV people. From time to time on social media I still see the sort of bigoted and small-minded comments that were common 20 years ago. However, even where I'm based, which is far from cosmopolitan or particularly tolerant to difference, when asked how they experience living in this part of the world, my GV clients have all reported that it's fairly comfortable for them to go about their lives and they are pretty much left untroubled. I do consider myself to be quite blessed as I know that this isn't the case for many GV people both within these shores and overseas.

I'm reminded though that we still have some distance to travel to a time where we don't have binary or GV, and gender is commonly accepted as diverse with permutations that are equally valid.

I don't think it's fair to say that GV folk are playing fast and loose with the fundamentals of gender; however, I do believe that both they and those who fall under the category of cissexual have responsibilities in ensuring that future generations have the scope to align themselves with gender in a way that allows for a richer articulation of our self-identity.

Reflections on the Exercises

Over the years of training counsellors and therapists it has never ceased to strike me that I will meet some great practitioners, with many years of client experience behind them, who have never questioned their own GI. There is such pressure to ensure trainee counsellors are properly trained to meet the demands of clinical practice and have the expertise to help whoever walks into their counselling room that it is deeply concerning that GI mostly gets left off the training programme. There are some training establishments that include GI in their training material, but they are very much in the minority. Given this lack of clinical grounding for meeting and working with future GV clients, it feels important to me to get you thinking about your own GI.

As I'm sure you will have figured out by now, the exercises I have provided in this book are not the sort to demand a 'yes' or 'no' response. I'm hopeful we may have more shades of grey and not so much black and white. These exercises are meant to always reinforce the message that we're all a bit intersex hormonally. This can be a great leveller, and to an extent what it does is go beyond diversity and state that regardless of how differently we present on the outside we are more alike within. Below is a summary of the exercises so far.

Exercise 1: How Was Your Gender Identity Shaped?

As we have seen throughout this book, there is huge pressure placed upon us by external forces to be something we might not be. This pressure comes from both the wider society and our immediate family. These forces can be explicit in terms of social rules (e.g. a man should always hold the door open for a woman, or a man should give up his seat on a train/bus for a woman). Other forces can be implicit, such as we saw with the CoW and ELoE. These social forces have blurred edges at times. Take tomboys as an example: they have always been pretty much accepted as cute and quirky, and people tend to think it's just a phase the child will grow out of. But woe betide the boy who plays with dolls and wants to engage in activities that are socially regarded as female. And as for our supposed adult roles, might it not be healthier and more generally polite to hold the door open behind you for whoever is following you – a common courtesy to your fellow humans? Or if it looks like someone is struggling on the bus or train, should we not give them a helping hand or offer them a seat if it looks like they need it more than us – rather than just blindly following some archaic social rule?

This exercise is aimed to get you thinking about how much you are the captain of your own ship in your life and how much you have allowed other sources to knock you off your own natural course. That need for approval and acceptance is understandable for a child, but those external needs are not so easy to shake off once we enter into adult life. So, give some thought for a minute to the question: 'What have you given up of yourself merely to please others?' This can be quite sobering.

Exercise 2: Personal Meaning – Part 1

By the time we reached this exercise we had seen that GI is not the same as physical sex (our body). Despite physical sex markers (e.g. penis, breasts, vagina), the way an individual experiences themselves will not always align with these markers, and some people (non-binary) will not align with anything physical. With the beginnings of this broader GV vocabulary you were invited in this exercise to begin considering what male and female might be generally and personally and to ask yourself: 'What do you like about being who you are?' and 'If you enjoy being a man/woman, what is it about it that you like?' This built upon the unspoken gender shaping of Exercise 1. It asked you to start thinking more about what you are and what you are not, and maybe to uncover any wishes or desires to be freer in who you are; also to think about whether there are possibly things from other GIs which could be possibilities for you.

Exercise 3: An Exploration – The Dressing-Up Box

As we were able to see in Chapter 7, the GV individual experiences interest in 'forbidden fabrics' – textures, materials and specific gendered items – and the sensory relationship they have upon the skin. This becomes a fundamental experiential process by which the individual explores their physical selves. We saw this in the sections 'The Modes of Gendering and

Transgendering' and 'The Four Stages of Demystification of the Gender Variant Self-Image', where the client is now consciously undertaking a process of modifying their body in order to match their inner feelings with their outer self. There are several ways the GV individual can reflect on how they might match the many components and gender signifiers to their interpretation of their inner sensed self-image. This kind of exploration asks the client to actively appraise each aspect of themselves and to decide what part it plays in their overall self-image composition.

'The Dressing-Up Box' exercise is a nod to this initial interest in 'forbidden fabrics' and other such items which you might not have considered previously. It also asks you to consider the relationship of items that might be forbidden to you just because you were born on the other side of the gender border. Remember, clothes are genderless; it's the meaning and restrictions we place upon them that make them forbidden. It might be worth going back to this exercise whilst you look at the R.I.C.E.S. in 'The Modes of Gendering and Transgendering', and consider that many of these modes are not exclusive to GV individuals and that there may be some which you are already doing.

Let's pause for a moment and revisit the R.I.C.E.S.

Redefining – the individual's personal dialogue with and of themselves. The client's own understanding/interpretation of them self, which is based in the phenomena of them gendering their self.

Well, this is something that we all do. It's how one regards oneself and makes sense of oneself even if one sees oneself as being in line with the binary. You probably have an idea of whether you are a manly man or a girlie girl.

Implying – a process of indicating specific gender signifiers of the intended sex, i.e. wearing 'Breast Forms' or placing something in underpants as a substitute penis 'Packing'.

'Concealing'– a sub process of hiding body parts, e.g. 'Binding Breasts', 'Tucking Penis & Testicles'.

It is commonplace in society that if an individual is unhappy with some aspect of their physical self they can choose to undertake some form of cosmetic surgery, from breast enlargements, Botox fillers, hair implants and tanning to 'nip and tuck'. The choice and options of how to imply or conceal aspects of our bodies are accepted and barely questioned.

Erasing – eliminating aspects of the physical body which aren't identified with either personally or with the physical sex which the individual identifies with, e.g. growing hair, cutting hair, shaving body hair, wearing a hair piece, wearing/ not wearing makeup, etc.

If I say 'personal grooming', I think that is something which many of us can relate to. I don't think I need to say more.

Substituting – dressing style, posture, gesture, speech. The degrees to which the individual undertakes this will depend on varying factors such as age, positions on the continuum, if and how they are 'out', and finances to achieve some of the other aspects within R.I.C.E.S.

Again, these aspects of self are something we do and add to the overall composition of how we feel about ourselves and what we want to communicate about ourselves.

Being GV isn't 'dressing up' to some fantasy, yet it *is* about 'dressing towards' the GV individual's natural self. For many of us, the wish to dress up is something we will do for fun. Fancy-dress costumes have become quite state of the art, and many people like to dress up to mark a special occasion and to feel good. And although R.I.C.E.S. are an essential part of a GV individual's process towards actualisation, the feelgood factor is more of a safeguarding of their mental well-being.

Exercise 4: Personal Meaning – Part 2

I started by saying:

> So, to get you thinking about this process, I am going to present you with the following thoughts.

Our identity: How do we know who we are?

This exercise begins with the assumption that we know who we are or accept that we have an idea of who we are. We wake up every morning and know or expect to see there will be consistent traits that define us and make us the person we are. The exercise goes on to maintain that while these traits are part of us, we might not necessarily like them: some we value, whilst others we may be indifferent towards. The key is consistency – these traits are present throughout our lives and without effort.

> We are who we are... And for the most part we accept that. We may not like certain parts of ourselves; however, we know, understand and accept that they are part of us. The same applies to the parts we recognise as aspects we enjoy or like about ourselves. Both facets are carried with us over the course of our life. Sometimes they change, yet overall they are consistent in their presentation as part of us. So, another question I would like to offer for your consideration is:

How do you know what makes you...you?

How many of us have ever spent time reflecting on these types of questions? The exercise invites you to enlighten your knowledge of how you experience yourself in a perceptible manner. It asks you to consider your ontological experience, and how you interpret this as your personal truth of self. The exercise goes on to say:

> It's important to clarify that what I'm asking here is not about knowing your likes and dislikes – these are easier to figure out, and they are not the things I am asking you to contemplate.

I clarify here that what is being sought is not the surface stuff, although our likes and dislikes are obviously valid aspects of ourselves. These things can change throughout our lives and I class them as 'transient phenomena'. An interesting illustration is that of a friend who asked me some years after I had transitioned, 'So what kind of food do you eat now and do you find that you have a different taste in music now you live full-time as female?'

Now this might seem like a perfectly normal or perfectly obtuse question, depending on how you have understood the question asked by this exercise. What it does show is how delicate a process it is to sift the consistent from the transient phenomena.

Therefore, what I propose to make this process practicable is to apply the Phenomenological Method to peel back a few layers of your inner self and ask as a means of a starting position how you know you are the GI you are.

This exercise is a leveller. It shows us what our personal traits are. We come to recognise our consistent characteristic phenomena, and the process will be the same for us all, regardless of whether we are binary or GV. The exercise ends with a nod to a rather tantalising uncertainty which we all might wish to consider wherever we are on the gender continuum:

How can you be sure of anything you believe/d or sense/d about yourself?

Exercise 5: Personal Meaning – Part 3

This final exercise asked:

What kind of woman are you?

Or

What kind of man are you?

Exercise 5 invites you to bring together all the information you have uncovered during the four previous exercises and to consider what that says about you and how you do gender. Or maybe it brings up something completely different. Maybe it reinforces what you already know and, if so, that's great. Even if that's the case, perhaps it makes you reflect upon the way you do male or female: Are you closer to the hegemonic male or the emphasised female? If neither, that leads to the question: What's your version of gender binary? Alternatively, perhaps you have caught a small glimpse of something you hadn't seen before (I've referred to it as 'the uncanny'). If so, what is it that you have caught a glimpse of? Maybe this is something you might want to explore further? If that is the case, I would suggest that you go back and repeat the exercises, but this time incorporate the material you gathered the first time around – you can use it as your starting point in the processes and see what this brings up for you.

Whatever the outcome of the exercises, I believe this personal exploration is fundamentally important for us as counsellors – we need to have undertaken some exploration of this aspect of ourselves if we are to be effective in the counselling room with our GV clients. Whilst I agree it is important to be open with GV clients in that we may not know certain terminology and language (and as we have seen, openness and honesty are always the best policy here), I think that for us in our therapeutic roles it really isn't acceptable to never have checked out such a fundamental aspect of ourselves. If we have undertaken a personal exploration, it can only be beneficial to our clients in that it gives the message that even if we are cis we regard gender and GV to be important enough to warrant a personal inventory. And as we will see below, an unchecked gender could be seen as reinforcement of cissexual privilege/prejudice, and this will not aid the function of trust within therapeutic work. So, let us now look at the working of a model of therapy called 'Gender-Positive Therapy'.

Towards a Gender-Positive Therapeutic Model

What is 'Gender-Positive'? Well, it means having respect for, and acceptance of, people who identify as being somewhere on the transgendered spectrum. Historically, medical service providers pathologised and didn't take seriously those with gender dysphoria and GV. This is now regarded as a form of transphobia, and it bred suspicion and a lack of trust in the medical and therapeutic worlds. Although things have improved considerably over the last few years, I still hear of situations where therapists and medical professionals are making mistakes which run counter to the current progress towards regarding GV people as genuine and equally valid members of society. I received a message recently from a transsexual woman in her early thirties whose counsellor asked her for her deadname (the counsellor has only known the client as a transsexual woman, so why does the deadname matter to the work that they are engaged in?). This is an insensitive and trust-challenging matter and I could totally understand where the client was coming from when they said this had impacted their trust with the counsellor and they didn't feel secure in this therapeutic relationship.

Hypervigilance

Experiences like the one outlined above cause suspicion within the GV population and are seen as abusive by GV individuals who experienced them. This has resulted in GV individuals becoming hypervigilant in any situation that shows signs of hostility or misunderstanding. A simple act can be seen as invalidating the legitimate existence of a GV individual.

Hypervigilance might manifest itself in the form of the client asking quite direct questions about your understanding/feelings around GI. As therapeutic practitioners we will all need to be ethically and morally responsive to the needs and concerns of this diverse client group, yet at the same time not underestimating the restrictions that have been placed upon GV people in pursuit of determining their healthcare needs. Think for a moment about how you would react to a GV client asking you questions around your understanding of GV. To avoid or reflect back might not be the best option in this case and I always advise when working with this client group to not shy away from being honest and open. So, if you don't know, then say so. Trying to blag your way out of the situation will not be helpful and will again result in poor development of trust. Working with this client group is at times not for the faint-hearted and I would suggest that once you have read what I propose in this chapter you will need to decide if your clinical practice is suitable for this kind of approach.

As I see it, our therapeutic role is underpinned by the principles of enabling the client to gain a greater understanding within the four areas below (may I remind you to please reflect on how the Phenomenological Method may assist you with these enquiries):

1. How one experiences one's inner self.

2. How the world perceives one's outer self.

3. Sexual orientation (who one is sexually or romantically attracted to).

4. Sexual (orientation) identity.

An aspect of the work focuses on how these four ways of being-in-the-world mutually impact on one another. The overall aim is to facilitate the client to reach full integration into a consolidated self-actualisation. A hoped-for outcome of the work is the affirmation and validation (of and by the client) towards their gender and for them to achieve some comfort with their current body configuration. This could itself diminish guilt/shame and enhance self-esteem in the client.

Transphobia within the context of the professional working relationship between clinician and client can be defined as: 'Any belief, attitude, act or behaviour which negatively values, denies, undermines, discourages or disempowers trans-identified clients in terms of their unique identities and subjective realities' (WPATH 2012).

Transpositivity aims to challenge transphobia with:

- positive values

- affirming

- supportiveness

- encouragement

- empowerment.

The GV community has a deep-rooted mistrust of mental health providers due to transphobic attitudes (both historic and current) such as this:

> Some things said to me at my last appointment (specifically that I should accept that my wife and daughters would be better off if I left them) upset me greatly. I left the GIC and sat in the car crying for over an hour. I decided there and then never to go back. (McNeil *et al.* 2012, p.32)

The Therapeutic Relationship

Bearing the above in mind, the professional working relationship between counsellor and client should ideally be collaborative, with scope for the therapist to act as an advocate for the client. This way of working is common outside the UK, where a therapist will often act as a 'gatekeeper' (i.e. the client's progression through the layers of medical services is supported by the therapist). In the UK the involvement/roles of counsellors and psychotherapists is less clear, and at times vague.

GV clients may access therapy for the following reasons:

- Own motivation – self-exploration.

- Non-GI matters.

- Contemplative (exploring their gender, with a view to transitioning).

- They have been requested to do so as part of the transition process by the GIC (maybe the medical services are not convinced the client is ready to begin the medical transition, or there are aspects of the client's life which give the medical professionals cause for concern as to the client's ability to manage the step over the gender border).

- Similar to the point above, the GIC may request the client to have therapy as part of the 'Real Life Test' if the client has experienced (or appears to have experienced) certain difficulties during this part of the transition process.

Advocacy, Alliance-Building and the Therapeutic Relationship

The therapist as advocate might feel like a major departure for most therapists. Yet I believe that this is possible with the following things in place:

- Firm boundaries.

- Informed knowledge.

- Clear client/therapist contracting.

- Regular reviewing. (Again I remind you of the need for strong boundaries.)

Clearly the need for this proposed role will depend on the client's presenting issue, and if they are transitioning and experiencing blocks or issues with the medical services. It is important to note that there won't always be the requirement to introduce the role of advocacy into the work.

If the client is looking to move towards a clinical transition, they will be accessing medical services, so now might be the time to introduce the role of collaborative advocacy if you and the client believe that this will help them through the process, or if they have limited support generally within their life. The client and therapist would be working as a scaled-down version of a multi-disciplinary team, each being clear about their respective roles within the therapeutic process and presenting a therapeutic alliance. If the client and therapist think that this is a good idea, a contract of advocacy will need to be outlined and agreed. Put simply:

- The GV client's role is to describe their experience in terms of 'being in the world', exploring and determining themselves and their needs.

- The therapist's role is, with the client's agreement (and contracting), to observe and reflect on the client's experiences, and to liaise with the clinical services if and when this is deemed by both client and therapist to be appropriate (the therapist is thus taking the role of healer/advocate).

Advocacy could mean contracted clinical work, such as providing the medical services with appropriate, boundaried and client-agreed updates on the therapeutic work undertaken; or it could mean the therapist will liaise with the medical services if the client is having difficulties with the GIC. This is not such a strange concept as it might first appear – with the introduction of the Gender GP service there is now an alternative service for accessing hormones at a more affordable rate.

Advocacy could also act as a function of social activism and role-modelling for the client. There are a lot of GV folk out there who are struggling to be taken seriously, from how they experience their GI through to wanting to manifest their identity in the world. The therapist's acceptance of the client and their narrative is a powerful display of belief in the individual, who is highly likely to have experienced a lot of challenges to their identity and who they are. This acceptance could be the beginning of them valuing themselves and could lead them to develop self-advocacy skills.

The WPATH *Standards of Care* (2012) talk about the therapeutic relationship between the counsellor and the GV individual as being a 'best fit' approach to treatment. The following points come to my mind whilst thinking about best fit.

- When working gender-positively, 'best fit' means putting the therapeutic contract to the test in terms of collaborative working within the guidelines I have mentioned above. It requires the willingness of the therapist and client to be open to honest negotiation around the *Standards of Care*.

- The therapist includes and accepts reasonable requests for the treatment made by the client, and the client accepts realistic limits to the treatment according to clinical discretion. (Sometimes the GV individual may have beliefs about what can be achieved medically beyond what is medically realistic.)

- Gender-positive therapy within the clinical context implies a collaborative working relationship based on mutual trust, respect and flexibility, with a joint commitment to operate in good faith.

- Objectives for client-directed counselling/psychotherapy aim to foster development towards the self-actualisation and self-empowerment of the client.

- Remember to always keep 'client centredness' at the forefront of your mind and work with an individual treatment plan. The *Standards of Care* for the guidelines of patient care say: 'No two transsexuals are the same in terms of their personal expectations' (WPATH 2012).

There are currently very few specific Gender-Positive Therapy models for gender dysphoria. However, by taking an integrative approach, the therapist stands a better chance of reaching a sensitive and gender-affirming approach to the client's needs.

Let us now turn to clinical orientation and Gender-Positive Therapy.

Clinical Orientation/Treatment Philosophy

Firstly, don't assume that because you know you work in a client/person-centred way the client will know this. Working with GV, the usual rules apply as with any new client work. However, as mentioned above, you are likely to be working with some hypervigilant clients, so what we usually encounter with clients at the beginning of a piece of work (i.e. building up mutual trust) might be a little harder than normal. The work will demand that we pay attention to the therapeutic conditions of empathy, caring, sensitivity, validating, acceptance, compassion and supportiveness.

Remember you are likely to be this person's first positive experience of acceptance and belief in themselves. As I have mentioned throughout this book, it is essential that we are mindful of the language we use with our GV clients as it might not take much to damage an already fragile trust. If in doubt, admit you don't know and ask the client what is okay to say.

You may encounter a client who has already stepped over the gender border and is living full-time. Alternatively, they have only just begun their Real Life Experience (RLE). The *Standards of Care* (WPATH 2012) say that the individual must usually live full-time in their identified gender for a minimum of a year.

The RLE is supposed to remove any lingering doubts about whether an individual is totally prepared for the irreversible impact of SRS and is sure of their GI. It is seen as a real-life rehearsal.

However, the RLE is seen as quite controversial by some transsexuals. How does the psychiatrist interpret whether the client has had a successful experience and is ready to move on to the next stage of medicalised treatment (usually hormones)? If the individual does not have what the psychiatrist would deem a successful RLE (and therefore doesn't think that the individual is ready for the next stage of the transition), what does that say about the transsexual, their situation and the feelings they have regarding their gender? Are they then not GV? Or are they just not GV enough? This is a difficult situation for the client to find themselves in.

Therapy is something which isn't always needed or required by GV people – much like anyone else really. However, for those who do wish to access Gender-Positive Therapy, it should be made available prior to and during the transitional process and, if required, post-transition too. In the view of trans-supportive clinicians, the view of therapy is not to cure cross-gender identification/dysphoria (as is believed to be the case by some theologically backed therapists); rather it's to assist individuals to function more comfortably in the world with their identified GI, through a process of exploration, consolidation and actualisation.

We as therapists working with GV clients must exercise vigilance around potential counter-transference issues which arise during therapy. An example of this would be 'over-encouragement', where the therapist finds themselves overly steering the work towards a particular outcome of change for the client. This might take the form consciously or otherwise, of placing emphasis on the client to relinquish his or her transsexual self-identity, or the pursuit of sex reassignment (changing one's sex/body) as opposed to adopting a GI (changing one's gender identity) and/or sexual identity (gay, lesbian, bisexual). Remaining clear in our minds as to how we are reacting to the client's narrative is paramount as we walk with them whilst they find what is right for them.

Due to the diversity of the gender population, and the individual's specific needs, it is essential for the therapist to be aware of the various permutations and outcomes that clients may desire and request as part of their GI. As we know, not all GV individuals are the same and some may require more medical and therapeutic input than others to achieve lasting personal comfort with their gendered selves. The variations of possible desired outcomes are sex hormones and SRS, unless the person identifies as non-operative. There will be some transsexuals who might only want hormones and no surgery, and there will be others who might want no form of medical intervention. Transsexual does not constitute hormones and surgery.

Concerns about Working with This Client Group – Questions and Answers

Q I don't think I can include advocacy in my client work and advocate for the client. It's not what I'm trained in and I don't see how this fits with my clinical approach. Don't I need to be a specially trained GI therapist?

A Obviously when asking yourself these questions, give consideration to the BACP *Ethical Framework for the Counselling Professions*, in particular the values and principles of counselling and psychotherapy:

- Respecting human rights and dignity.

- Protecting the safety of clients.

- Ensuring the integrity of practitioner–client relationships.

- Enhancing the quality of professional knowledge and its application.

- Alleviating personal distress and suffering.

- Fostering a sense of self that is meaningful to the person(s) concerned.

- Increasing personal effectiveness.

- Enhancing the quality of relationships between people.

- Appreciating the variety of human experience and culture.

- Striving for the fair and adequate provision of counselling and psychotherapy services.

(BACP 2018, p.9)

Also:

- Being trustworthy: honouring the trust placed in the practitioner (also referred to as fidelity).

- Autonomy: respect for the client's right to be self-governing.

- Beneficence: a commitment to promoting the client's well-being.

- Non-maleficence: a commitment to avoiding harm to the client.

- Justice: the fair and impartial treatment of all clients and the provision of adequate services.

- Self-respect: fostering the practitioner's self-knowledge and care for self.

(BACP 2018, p.9)

These are principles we are introduced to at the very beginning of our careers. Unless a specific event occurs in our clinical life, which prompts us to revisit them, we probably don't think about these principles a great deal – not because we don't care about them but rather because they have become second-nature to us and we find ourselves just doing them as part of how we are as practitioners. If you were asked to do something clinically that didn't feel right and ethical to you, what would you do? What I am putting before you are options to consider. And as we have seen earlier, advocacy might mean providing some form of written acknowledgement of the work undertaken that the client can show to medical practitioners. I'm wondering if that is something that you might already do in some capacity in your client work. Remember you are a counsellor, psychotherapist or some other therapist and that is your specialty. If you remain within that role, you are going to be doing what it is you do. If you are reading this book, it could possibly mean that you have an interest in this particular field; I have included information in this book that I believe will supplement your clinical approach, and it is important to remember that I have experience from both positions of client and therapist, so I am aware of the traps and pitfalls that GV folk encounter along their journey. It is my belief that as long as the advocacy aspect of the client work is clearly contracted, and all permissions granted, this element can run smoothly. Let us remind ourselves of the emphasis of WPATH's *Standards of Care* and see how that fits in with our roles as therapists:

> To provide clinical guidance for health professionals to assist transgender, transsexuals, and gender non-conforming people with safe and effective pathways to lasting personal comfort with their gendered selves, in order to maximise their overall health, psychological well-being, and self-fulfilment. (WPATH 2012, p.1)

Now let us focus for a moment on that last part of the sentence: 'in order to maximise their overall health, psychological well-being, and self-fulfilment'. This feels like what underpins the client work I undertake, regardless of whether it is focused on GI or not. What about you?

A lot of what I have been discussing within this book in relation to the Gender-Positive Therapy model is what you do with your clients already. GV clients want to be treated like any other. The information included within this book is a strong tool that can be built upon.

Returning to the question 'Do I need to be a specially trained therapist?' This depends on the level/depth of the work you are considering undertaking. Some GV clients will have needs which you are able to accommodate within your current skills base and competency, and there will be those with whom you might feel out of your depth. This book has addressed all the areas you are likely to encounter. Asking the client questions about what they see their needs as being, and what would constitute progress, will enable you to gauge if the client is presenting something you can ultimately work with. Finally, check out with yourself how you feel about the potential work, and like any other piece of client work, *know your limits*.

In conclusion, I will turn to two specific aspects of the BACP's *Ethical Framework for Good Practice*:

> Beneficence: a commitment to promoting the client's well-being.

> Non-maleficence: a commitment to avoiding harm to the client.

> *(BACP 2018, p.11)*

These are fundamental clinical points, of course. However, as we have seen throughout this book, GV clients unknowingly bring with them a minefield of moral and ethical challenges when they enter the counselling room. And to the counsellor inexperienced in working with GV, there are aspects within the work where we as professionals could unintentionally make mistakes.

Firstly, looking at beneficence, we may know that we are committed to promoting the well-being of the client. This might seem obvious, as surely our job is to help the client achieve their gender actualisation. Yet without careful exploration we could be pushing a client into a situation that they are not yet ready for, or that they are not physically or emotionally equipped to make. And in the worst case, we could put the client at risk of harm from others. The GV journey is a demanding road at the best of times and the client must be as prepared as possible for the outcomes from the choices they have and the decisions they make. An obvious example of poor beneficence would be a counsellor who overly enthusiastically, either through counter-transference or failing to hear and understand the client's unreadiness for transition, pushes the client over the transition border. The possible repercussions of this are many, but they all have one thing in common, and that is the client finding themselves either with regrets or facing unexpected challenges which they feel unable to manage. There is also the possibility that transition might be an avoidance of the individual's recognition that their sexuality is the concern (e.g. if they come from a homophobic background, changing gender might feel the lesser of two difficulties to deal with). And yes, this is something I have come across in my client work.

Turning our attention to non-maleficence, as well as including the possible implications covered with beneficence, we might impact the working relationship by lack of knowledge of GV etiquette. This would be considered to be maleficence, and examples of this are:

- Not asking, or assuming you know, whether the client is male, female or something else entirely.

- Not using the correct titles Mr, Miss, Ms, Mrs, Mx or something else entirely.

- Asking the client's deadname.

- Using the term 'tranny' at any time would be a bad idea.

- Showing incredulity if the client describes their gender as something you find hard to get your head around – this would be particularly relevant with genderqueer or non-binary clients. An example is the client who describes themselves as 'purple'.

- Making assumptions about the GV client in front of you because you have worked with GV clients previously and surely their needs are the same? Remember the Rule of Epoché from the Phenomenological Method and suspend all judgements, including previous GV client work.

- Dealing with hypervigilance calmly and effectively. Sometimes it's best to say you don't know if the client asks a direct question about your opinion of GV. I feel that to use the stock answer of 'We are not here to talk about me, this session is about you' may be heard as avoiding the subject and could lead the client to find it difficult to trust you.

I find that it is usually better to answer the question with an appropriate and considered reply.

As you can see from these examples, managing a potential *faux-pas* demands that we tread carefully and consider our interventions, as the risks of negatively affecting the therapeutic relationship are various and the impact could be far-reaching. The above list is what I consider we should be mindful of when working with GV. Exploring your own GI will certainly assist you with client work in this area, and will take you a step away from contributing to the 'us and them' status quo.

The End of the Beginning – Dare We Be Ourselves?

So here we are towards the end of this reflective process. We have seen that GV is widespread and normal in other species. We have seen how societal changes, from hunter-gathering to agriculture, led to societies ultimately shifting from an equal societal structure to a rigid and less forgiving one heavily influenced by patriarchy. This led not only to a false comprehension of gender but to the normalisation of the gender binary across many societies worldwide, where masculinity is now regarded as primary, strong and deserving of societal privilege and femininity is regarded as weak, secondary and without privilege. And if you don't fall into either of those categories? Well, then…God help you! We find ourselves in a world where for many of us GI has strict and unspoken rules, and there is an expectation by some that we should accept this as if they were part of social law. We have also seen that GV in the human species is nothing new. We are now at the beginning of a social era where we are openly discussing GV. For this to be a truly meaningful examination, we will need to consider gender itself rather than perpetuating an 'us and them' situation between GV and cissexualism. However, these healthy and unbiased examinations are not happening nearly enough. Other than the trainings which I have been delivering for the last six years, I've not come across any other trainings for therapists which consider the subject of GV in any other way than in an academic or fact and information fashion. This becomes a hindrance; until we begin considering the matter of gender being all-encompassing (i.e. affecting the entire poputlation of the planet) – rather than as we currently do by getting distracted in believing GV is the problem that demands a solution, rather than progressing towards a mindset where gender is automatically regarded as multifaceted and we can do away with terms such as 'cissexual' and 'gender variance' – we will continue to struggle with what I call 'the trouble with gender variance'.

My aim for this book wasn't for it to be solely a step-by-step guide of how to work clinically with GV clients, although I've given you, dear reader, some ideas for consideration and one or two suggestions of what might be helpful. My main aim was to address the issue of the trouble with GV, hence the need to look at the bigger picture, including GV in the natural world: If it's normal for GV to exist in other species, then why should humans be so different? It is also important to recognise that GV has been around since the dawn of time and has commonly existed. It has not only been widely accepted in various cultures throughout history, it has often been integral and intrinsically woven into the traditions and beliefs of those cultures. This is still the case in many non-Westernised societies today. The reflective exercises are my invitation to you, dear reader, to join in the next footsteps in bringing change to this quandary, 'the trouble with gender variance'. As I say during training sessions, this process of change is live and happening now. By bringing some of the therapeutic considerations covered in this book into your work, you will be assisting GV clients to find a meaningful understanding of their gender and to own their space on the gender continuum; and by engaging with the exercises yourself, you will be consciously and firmly taking your space on the gender continuum too. This matter concerns every one of us. As we have seen, we all inhabit a GI, and we owe a responsibility to ourselves and future generations to be engaged and to recognise the subtleties and nuances that make up the very essence of gender.

The May 2018 issue of *Therapy Today*, the British Association for Counselling and Psychotherapy's monthly journal, piqued my interest with an article exploring what gender means to all of us' (Moon, Ross and Wolton 2018, p.35). I was intrigued. However, I was rather thrown by the article's title, which was 'It's OK not to know about gender'. So what were they suggesting? A subheading goes on to state that 'therapists should feel able to admit to not knowing'. In terms of gender, the first thought that comes to mind is 'admitting this to who and in what context?' This isn't a problem in training or in your own personal therapy. While I think it's okay to not be sure of gender-related terminology (which is confusing) and it's appropriate to ask the client which pronoun they would like us to use, I think it would be unhelpful and damaging to admit to not understanding GI to a GV client within their therapy, especially as we all have one. Of course, I am very aware that as therapists the core of our work with clients is fundamentally based in the not or unknown, and that clients' and therapists' progress is always on the edge of awareness. However, with regard to something so profoundly part of us all, to work with GV and to not have questioned ourselves is negligent. It's imperative that we as therapists have questioned and explored ourselves. To be fair, the article does go on to say that 'sometimes we may need to explore our gender' (Moon *et al.* 2018, p.36). I would advocate that *we definitely do* need to explore our gender.

Despite my concerns, I welcome this article in bringing self-reflectiveness into the open. Its intentions are positive, yet the way it presents its propositions is disorganised, thus potentially adding to the confused fashion-ability that has become the current landscape of trans/transgender where the subject becomes reduced to an empty self-expressiveness, as we saw in cases mentioned earlier.

What troubles me is that the article appears to suggest that if you happen to know the right sort of questions to ask of yourself you will unveil your gender truth and the correct answer to who you are. The article talks about asking ourselves who our gendered self was as a child. During those formative years, I had no concept of my gendered self or even what a gendered self was! I experienced something about myself that carried immense shame and guilt. For the most part this was dark and perverse, as shown by the 'In Treatment' episodes of this book. My 'gendered self' question overlooks the fact that it was a different time, when these sorts of matters were best kept hidden for fear of the conscquences. My experiences are shared by many others living with the complexity of gender dysphoria. They are neither fond memories nor an experiential exercise – it felt like survival. Those suggested questions make the enquiry a simplified academic exercise rather than something that might meaningfully expose the fundamental essences of one's GI composition and possibly go some way to removing gender labels and borders.

Of course, we all have to start somewhere with our enquiry, and the exercises included in this book are aimed primarily at cissexual counsellors who are yet to unravel their gender, and it is not going to be achieved that simply. I see the exercises I've offered to be more like fishing in a deep, dark pool. You may cast your line and there is no way of knowing what, if anything, will surface. After many years of personal therapy, my gender is still unfolding. It's much more than a somatic and mental dilemma. It contains a spiritual component, much like it does for the indigenous cultures we have looked at. It is something that transcends my day-to-day life and yet it's part of all I do. It aids me in making sense of my personal history and presents me with a context that adds form to my history and how I am now. I have seen something similar within the many clients who experience a dysphoria around the split between their inner and outer selves. During my day-to-day life I don't abandon gender labels. I am Madison merely doing the things that Madison does. I chose not to engage in the labels which seem to be part of the hysteria that is fuelling the trouble with GV terminology. It was created by others and doesn't speak my truth. For 40 years of my life I fought desperately to find inner peace and to not only acknowledge my authentic self but to be able to live with authenticity.

I'm going to give the last words of this book to Julia Serano, an American writer, performer, lecturer, gender activist and speaker on the subjects of sex, gender and all things related. The first time I read this, it brought me to tears, as it spoke of a struggle that has silently gone on for the longest time all around the world for all the nameless GV people. In this piece Julia recognises that these individuals have been involved in their private struggles to be themselves. What I also like is her belief that there is no certainty when it comes to gender. Similar to what I say during my trainings on GI, I'll finish by saying: 'If I have done my job well, you should be more confused than when you started this book!'

Over to you, Julia:

Instead of saying that all gender is performance, let's admit that sometimes gender is an act, and other times it isn't. And since we can't get inside one another's minds, we have no way of knowing whether any given person's gender is sincere or contrived. Let's fess up to the fact that when we make judgements about other people's genders, we're typically basing it on our own assumptions (and we all know what happens when you assume, right?).

Let's stop claiming that certain genders and sexualities 'reinforce the gender binary.' In the past, that tactic has been used to dismiss butches and femmes, bisexuals, trans folks and their partners and feminine people of every persuasion. Gender isn't simply some faucet that we can turn on and off in order to appease other people, whether they be heterosexist bigots or queerer-than-thou hipsters. How about this: Let's stop pretending that we have all the answers, because when it comes to gender, none of us is fucking omniscient.

Instead of trying to fictionalise gender, let's talk about the moments in life when gender feels all too real. Because gender doesn't feel like drag when you're a young trans child begging your parents to not cut your hair or not force you to wear that dress. And gender doesn't feel like a performance when for the first time in your life, you feel safe and empowered enough to express yourself in ways that resonate with you, rather than remaining closeted for the benefit of others. And gender doesn't feel like a construct when you finally find that special person whose body, personality, identity, and energy feels like a perfect fit with yours. Let's stop trying to deconstruct gender into nonexistence, and instead start celebrating it as inexplicable, varied, profound, and intricate.

So, don't you dare dismiss my gender as construct, drag, or performance. My gender is a work of non-fiction. (Serano 2006, p.87)

REFERENCES

Anti-Defamation League (2003) 'The Pyramid of Hate Exercise.' USC Shoah Foundation Institute, University of Southern California. Available at sfi.usc.edu/sites/default/files/lessons/units/POH_Exercise_Final_0.pdf, accessed on 03/10/18.

APA (American Psychiatric Association) (1980) *Diagnostic and Statistical Manual of Mental Disorders, 3rd Edition* (DSM-III). New York, NY: American Psychiatric Publishing.

APA (American Psychiatric Association) (1987) *Diagnostic and Statistical Manual of Mental Disorders, 3rd Edition, Revised* (DSM-III-R). New York, NY: American Psychiatric Publishing.

APA (American Psychiatric Association) (2013) *Diagnostic and Statistical Manual of Mental Disorders, 5th Edition (DSM-5)*. New York, NY: American Psychiatric Publishing.

BACP (British Association for Counselling and Psychotherapy) (2018) *Ethical Framework for the Counselling Professions*. Lutterworth: BACP.

Bagemihl, B. (1999) *Biological Exuberance, Animal Homosexuality and Natural Diversity*. New York, NY: St Martin's Press.

Benjamin, H, (1999) *The Transsexual Phenomenon*. Available at www.mut23.de/texte/Harry%20Benjamin%20-%20The%20Transsexual%20Phenomenon.pdf, accessed on 12/11/18.

Blanchard, R. (1991) 'Clinical observations and systematic studies of autogynephilia.' *Journal of Sex and Marital Therapy 17*, 235–251.

Bornstein, K. (1998) *My Gender Workbook*. London: Routledge.

Bornstein, K. and Bergman, S. B. (2010) *Gender Outlaws: The Next Generation.* Berkeley, CA: Seal.

Carroll, L. (1865) *Alice's Adventures in Wonderland.* Chicago, IL: Volume One Publishing.

Clarke, A. (1974) *Penda's Fen.* BBC/The British Film Institute.

Collins English Dictionary (2015) Glasgow: HarperCollins.

Cooney, K. (2014) *The Woman Who Would Be King: Hatshepsut's Rise to Power in Ancient Egypt.* New York, NY: Random House.

Darwin, C. (1809) *On the Origin of the Species.* Oxford: Oxford University Press.

de Beauvoir, S. (2011) *The Second Sex.* New York, NY: Vintage Books.

Diamond, L. and Butterworth, M. (2014) *The Handbook of Identity Theory and Research.* New York, NY: Springer.

Docter, R. F. (2008) *Becoming a Woman: A Biography of Christine Jorgensen.* New York, NY: The Haworth Press.

Ekins, R. and King, D. (eds) (2006) *The Transgender Phenomena.* London: Sage.

Ellis, H. (1948) *Psychology of Sex,* 12th edition. London: Butterworth-Heinemann.

Escoffier, J. (2011) 'Imagining the she/male: Pornography and the transsexualisation of the heterosexual male.' Available at https://www.tandfonline.com/doi/abs/10.1080/15240657.2011.610230, accessed on 12/11/18.

Evans, D. (1996) *An Introductory Dictionary of Lacanian Psychoanalysis.* London: Routledge.

Feinberg, L. (1996) *Transgender Warriors: Making History from Joan of Arc to Dennis Rodman.* Boston, MA: Beacon Press.

Fenstermaker, S. and West, C. (2002) *Doing Gender, Doing Difference: Inequality, Power, and Institutional Change.* New York, NY: Routledge.

Foster, V. E. (2009) 'The passing of a trans icon.' *Trans Political BlogSpot.* Available at http://transpolitical.blogspot.co.uk/2009/05/virginia-prince-passing-of-trans-icon.html, accessed on 04/10/18.

Freud, S. (2001) *The Interpretation of Dreams – Part One.* London: Vintage Books.

Google online dictionary (2018) 'Self-expression.' Available at www.google.co.uk/search?q=Dictionary, accessed 04/10/18.

Gov.uk (n.d.) 'Apply for a Gender Recognition Certificate.' Available at https://www.gov.uk/apply-gender-recognition-certificate, accessed on 07/11/18.

Greer, G. (1999) *The Whole Woman.* London: Transworld Publishers.

Grosz, E. (1995) *Space, Time and Perversion: Essays on the Politics of Bodies.* London: Routledge.

Hayes-Light, J. (2017) 'Why not "disorders of sex development?"' The UK Intersex Association. Available at www.ukia.co.uk/ukia/dsd.html, accessed on 03/10/18.

Herdt, G. (1993) *Third Sex, Third Gender: Beyond Sexual Dimorphism in Culture and History*. New York, NY: Zone Books.

Hirschfeld, M. (1991) *Transvestites: The Erotic Drive to Cross-Dress*. New York, NY: Prometheus Books.

Holy Bible (1891) Authorised King James Version. London: Collins.

Kinsey, A. C., Pomeroy, W. B. and Martin, C. E. (1975) *Sexual Behavior in the Human Male*. Bloomington, IN: Indiana University Press.

Krafft-Ebing, R. (1997) *Psychopathia Sexualis: The Case Histories*. Creation Books.

Kulish, N. (1997) 'Primary femininity: Clinical advances and theoretical advances.' Available at citeseerx.ist.psu.edu/viewdoc/download?doi=10.1.1. 875.1832&rep=rep1&type=pdf, accessed on 03/10/18.

McNeil, J., Bailey, L., Ellis, S., Morton, J. and Regan, M. (2012) *Trans Mental Health Study 2012*. Edinburgh: Scottish Transgender Alliance.

Mearns, D. and Thorne, B. (1988) *Person Centred Counselling in Action*. London: Sage.

Medwed, R. (2015) 'More than just male and female: The six genders in Classical Judaism.' *Sojourn Blog*. Available at www.sojourngsd.org/blog/sixgenders, accessed on 04/10/18.

Money, J. (1986) *Lovemaps: Clinical Concepts of Sexual/Erotic Health and Pathology, Paraphilia, and Gender Transposition in Childhood, Adolescence, and Maturity*. New York, NY: Irvington.

Moon, I., Ross, M. and Wolton, A. (eds) (2018) 'It's OK not to know about gender.' *Therapy Today 29*, 4, 35–37.

Oliven, J. F. (1965) *Sexual Hygiene and Pathology: A Manual for the Physician and the Professions*. Philadelphia, PA: Lippincott.

Quran (2018) Sahih International translation. Available at https://quran.com/42/49-53?translations=20), accessed on 04/10/18.

Rapoport, E. (2009) 'Bisexuality in psychoanalytic theory: Interpreting the resistance.' *Journal of Bisexuality 9*, 3–4, 279–295. Available at https://radicalbi. files.wordpress.com/2012/12/bisexuality-in-psychoanalytic-theory.pdf, accessed on 08/11/18.

Roughgarden, J. (2004) *Evolution's Rainbow: Diversity, Gender, and Sexuality in Nature and People*. Berkeley and Los Angeles, CA: University of California Press.

ScienceDaily (2015) 'Networks of the brain reflect the individual gender identity.' Available at www.sciencedaily.com/releases/2015/01/150107082133.htm, accessed on 04/10/18.

Serano, J. (2006) *Whipping Girl: A Transsexual Woman on Sexism and the Scapegoating of Femininity*. Berkeley, CA: Seal Press.

Spinelli, E. (1989) *The Interpreted World: An Introduction to Phenomenological Psychology*. London: Sage.

Stoller, R. J. (1984) *Sex and Gender: The Development of Masculinity and Femininity.* London: Karnac.

Taylor, S. (2005) *The Fall: The Insanity of the Ego in Human History and the Dawning of a New Era*. Winchester: O-Books.

WPATH (World Professional Association for Transgender Health) (2012) *Standards of Care for the Health of Transsexual, Transgender, and Gender Nonconforming People*. Available at www.wpath.org/media/cms/Documents/Web%20 Transfer/SOC/Standards%20of%20Care%20V7%20-%202011%20WPATH. pdf, accessed on 04/10/18.

INDEX